W9-ADP-051

McGRAW-HILL
INDUSTRIAL ORGANIZATION AND MANAGEMENT SERIES
L. C. MORROW, *Consulting Editor*

MAKING CONFERENCE PROGRAMS WORK

McGRAW-HILL

INDUSTRIAL ORGANIZATION AND MANAGEMENT SERIES

L. C. MORROW, *Consulting Editor*
Editor, Factory Management and Maintenance

Assisted by a Board of Industrial and Educational Advisers

(*Books already published or in production*)

BENSON—*Music and Sound Systems in Industry*
BETHEL, ATWATER, SMITH, and STACKMAN—*Industrial Organization and Management*
BIKLEN and BRETH—*The Successful Employee Publication*
BRIDGES—*Job Placement of the Physically Handicapped*
CANTOR—*Employee Counseling*
CHEYFITZ—*Constructive Collective Bargaining*
DICKIE—*Production With Safety*
DRAKE and DRAKE—*A Human Relations Casebook for Executives and Supervisors*
ELLS—*Salary and Wage Administration*
EVANS—*A Program for Personnel Administration*
FERN—*Training for Supervision in Industry*
FITZPATRICK—*Understanding Labor*
GARDINER—*When Foreman and Steward Bargain*
GILBRETH and COOK—*The Foreman in Manpower Management*
GRANT—*Statistical Quality Control*
HANNAFORD—*Conference Leadership in Business and Industry*
HILL—*Pattern for Good Labor Relations*
HILL and HOOK—*Management at the Bargaining Table*
HYDE—*Fundamentals of Successful Manufacturing*
KALSEM—*Practical Supervision*
KIMBALL and KIMBALL—*Principles of Industrial Organization and Management*
LAWSHE—*Principles of Personnel Testing*
LINCOLN—*Lincoln's Incentive System*
LIPPERT—*Accident Prevention Administration*
MAYNARD, STEGEMERTEN, and SCHWAB—*Methods-Time Measurement*
MORGAN—*Industrial Training and Testing*
NEUSCHEL and JOHNSON—*How to Take Physical Inventory*
PRESGRAVE—*The Dynamics of Time Study*
SEINWERTH—*Getting Results from Suggestion Plans*
SMITH—*Control Charts*
SMYTH and MURPHY—*Job Evaluation and Employee Rating*
STIGERS—*Making Conference Programs Work*
STOWERS—*Management Can Be Human*
THOMPSON—*Engineering Organization and Methods*
TOOTLE—*Employees Are People*
WIREN and HEYEL—*Practical Management Research*
YOUNG—*Personnel Manual for Executives*

Making Conference Programs Work

BY

M. F. STIGERS

Associate Professor of
Trade and Industrial Education
Purdue University
Teacher Trainer, Conference Leader, and
Conference Leader Trainer

First Edition

NEW YORK TORONTO LONDON

McGRAW-HILL BOOK COMPANY, INC.

1949

MAKING CONFERENCE PROGRAMS WORK

PREFACE

Experience has proved the value of conferences in the modern American way of life. Wherever problems affecting two or more people have required an answer, the conference procedure has been found to be the best method for working out the needed solution. In this country problems affecting two or more persons occur many times daily in industry, in commercial organizations, in public schools, colleges, and universities, in religious organizations—in fact, wherever a number of people are banded together to do a part of the world's work. The importance of conferences for dealing with these problems is being increasingly recognized.

A modern conference is not conducted according to parliamentary rules, as is the National Congress in Washington, D. C., the state legislatures, or the United Nations Assembly. Today's conference is informal, but it must be carefully planned and skillfully conducted. It requires a competent leader, one who has mastered the techniques of conference leadership.

It is now recognized that competent leaders, who are so essential for successful conferences, can result only from effective training of conference leaders. However, a search of text materials discloses no clean-cut technique for the training of conference leaders. Much has been written regarding the importance of conferences, the qualifications of a conference leader, the techniques of conference leadership, teaching by means of conferences, and planning for conferences. But there is a definite need for text material that tells how a conference leader or a group of leaders should be trained.

It is possible for an individual to acquire some skill in conference leadership without the services of a trainer, but it is a long, tedious, and costly experience. Many a potentially skillful conference leader may acquire some skills and some moderate success by working alone, but he will probably never progress to the point where he knows and can use the finer techniques that would put him in the top bracket, that would give him a deserved reputation as a skilled conference leader, and that would help him to serve his organization most effectively.

One of the purposes of this text is to furnish a guide for the training of student conference leaders by an experienced leader. Even though the experienced conference leader may not have trained student leaders previously, he can, by following the steps outlined in this text, improve his own skill in conference leadership and successfully train other persons to become competent conference leaders. The training procedures presented have been used successfully in training hundreds of leaders in many organizations, both industrial and educational.

The second purpose of this text is to present suggestions concerning how to make the best use of conferences, how to fit a conference program into an organization-wide training and education program. Many organizations, most of them industrial, are using conferences without a well-matured plan. Because they have heard that conferences are helpful in solving various problems and that conferences are an evidence of progressiveness, they have "climbed on the bandwagon," hoping and expecting that by this action alone most of their troubles would be easily solved and would remain solved. Very few of these hastily begun conference programs have netted some substantial results. These had the good fortune to have been well planned and carried out by experienced leaders, or by very good potential leaders. But these few successes are overshadowed by many programs that began with great enthusiasm and energy but lacked practical and long-range planning and which lacked understanding of those factors enabling a conference program to fit smoothly into existing procedures and organizational setup. The failures of these programs have caused participants to lose faith in conference procedures and have caused other organizations to decide not to embark on programs of their own.

It is often as important to know how to use a tool as it is to possess it. It is for the purpose of helping people to acquire a tool and of suggesting how to use it effectively that this text is written.

The author wishes to make a few heartfelt statements. After having conducted thousands of conferences and having been a participant in many more, and after having trained hundreds of men and women in the techniques of leading conferences, he can truthfully say that he has gained from this work more thrills and more satisfaction from observing individuals grow in understanding and in ability, gained more satisfaction from seeing proof of the success of conference programs, and gained more useful knowledge and ability for himself than he gained in any of the other work experiences he has ever had. The author wishes to acknowledge the many lasting friendships his work has made possible for him, both in schools and in industry, and in an area comprising many of the Middle Western states. He hopes that many, many more organizations and countless men and women may be influenced to acquire and use this tool that builds greater ability and character for the individual and promotes better teamwork and more efficient operation within their organization.

M. F. Stigers

Evansville, Ind.
January, 1949

CONTENTS

Part 1

INFORMATION SHEETS; HOW TO TRAIN CONFERENCE LEADERS

CHAPTER 1

INTRODUCTION

The first part of this text is presented as a guide for the training of conference leaders. It is actually a course of study taught by an instructor to a group of students. The instructor in this case is an experienced conference leader and conference-leader trainer, and the students are mature individuals chosen to receive training in conference leadership. Emphasis is placed on thorough preparation by the conference-leader trainer in order that he may effectively train key persons in the mastery of a valuable training and problem-solving device. Emphasis is likewise placed on thorough preparation by the student conference leaders in order that they may effectively participate in the various steps or operations.

Too often the training of conference leaders is attempted casually or haphazardly by a person not well qualified as a trainer. He may be intelligent and able in many ways, but may lack experience in conference leadership and in knowledge of how to train others in the use of this skill. Too often the persons selected to be student conference leaders have not been well chosen in that not everyone can be successfully trained to be an effective conference leader in the usually short and intensive training period provided. This does not necessarily mean that those persons who are not suitable for training lack intelligence or ability, but it does mean that the choice of student conference leaders should be in keeping with the requirements for successful conference leadership.

For a successful conference training program there is another consideration to be emphasized. Sometimes persons chosen to be trained as conference leaders have responsible positions entailing duties that require their full time and attention. They are expected to find the time to take the conference-leader training and later to lead successful conferences while still discharging all former duties. This is both unwise and unfair. It is unwise in that a person with too heavy a load will usually slight, and not necessarily intentionally, one or more of his duties and responsibilities. Slighting a duty or responsibility is costly in many ways. Poorly conducted conferences lead to lowering of employee morale, to lack of confidence in the leader and in the organization, and to continuation of the conditions the conferences were intended to remedy. Adding the responsibility of preparing for and leading conferences on top of an already full load is unfair in that the organization employing the person will profit the most by the exercise of the added responsibility and should therefore be willing to provide for the added responsibility on company time. This will probably mean that in those cases where conference leadership is added to an already full load, some of the former duties will be removed or the person involved will be permitted to delegate some of his former personal duties to one of his subordinates.

As an aid to both conference-leader trainers and student conference leaders, the text includes standard items used by experienced instructors. Examples of these items are course objectives, course outlines, and information sheets. Included, also, are devices or items peculiar to the needs of this course, such as samples of problem statements, conference objectives, definitions, opening statements, and conference discussion outlines. Still other items are classifications of conference problems, samples of the minutes or reports of conferences, and a student conference-leader rating form.

Since students learn by doing, a course in conference leadership requires the student leader to lead practice conferences. The number of practice conferences required to enable the student to lead successful work conferences varies from person to person. The problem of the number of practice conferences is discussed later in the text.

Practice conferences preferably are conducted with a group of student leaders. The student leader in such a practice conference has a sympathetic and cooperative group to work with. The setting and atmosphere of such a group make it easier for a timid or retiring individual to lead his first conference. Even this admittedly favorable situation is alarming and fearsome to some people, and now and then a well-educated, or at least a talented, individual is seized with stage fright and refuses to continue his training. It is regrettable, but it happens. Therefore care must be taken to make the beginning as easy and matter of fact as possible.

In the following pages the mechanics or devices for practice conferences are provided, the minimum number of such practice conferences being at the discretion of those in charge of the program. After the minimum number of practice conferences (discussed later in the text), the new leader is ready to conduct work conferences; with additional experience he will continue to grow in confidence and in his ability to use this very valuable modern tool.

OVER-ALL OR ULTIMATE OBJECTIVES FOR CONFERENCE LEADERSHIP TRAINING

The aim or ultimate purpose in offering a course in conference leadership is to aid in meeting the demand in both schools and industry for persons skilled in the leading of conferences. This training is definitely intended to prepare the potential leader to lead conferences successfully regardless of the educational background of the conferees and the nature of the problem or topic for discussion.

SPECIFIC OBJECTIVES FOR CONFERENCE LEADERSHIP COURSE

1. To understand what a conference is, what its advantages are, and when it should be used.

2. To understand the techniques and etiquette of conference leadership.

3. To understand the physical setup for a conference and the reasons for such a setup.

4. To understand what constitutes a conference problem or topic and what may be the sources for problems and topics.

5. To select a problem and prepare definitions, objectives, and a preliminary statement.

6. To prepare a discussion plan or outline.

7. To lead the practice conference and to acquire an appreciation of the techniques involved.

8. To lead other conferences, profiting by experience and acquiring additional skill and confidence.

CHAPTER 2

THE WHAT, WHEN, AND WHERE OF A CONFERENCE

DEFINITIONS OF A CONFERENCE AND DISCUSSION OF DEFINITIONS

1. A conference is a meeting where a number of people discuss the varying aspects of a given problem.
2. A conference is an educational medium consisting principally of a systematic, though informal, thinking through of a problem by a group of experienced persons.
3. A conference is an intelligently planned informal discussion of a problem, the discussion being participated in by a number of interested and/or experienced persons and supervised by a trained leader, with the purpose of reaching a useful conclusion or result.
4. A conference is a college seminar in overalls.

There is a reason for the inclusion of each of the four definitions given, although one of them is better than the others. The statements given in the first two are true, and each has been offered by many persons as their definition of a conference. However, these definitions are too brief and incomplete. They do not state all the important points regarding a conference. In order to bring out this deficiency, they should be compared with the third definition. In this third definition, note that a conference is a *discussion of a problem,* the discussion being *intelligently planned and informal;* the participants are persons having *interest in and experience with* the problem; the discussion is supervised by a *trained leader;* and there is the purpose of reaching a *useful conclusion or result.* By making this detailed study and comparison of the first three definitions, it becomes clear that the first two are incomplete and in what respect they are incomplete. The shortcomings of the first two in comparison with the third are quite evident.

The fourth definition is included to illustrate the fact that many a good and effective conference has for its participants persons with limited formal schooling, persons wearing rough work clothing showing evidence of direct contact with machines and materials. A good and effective conference is not limited to men and women who are college-trained and who wear fine clothing. The clothing is no sure indication of the quantity of formal schooling, nor is it a sure indication of the quality of a person's thinking.

In conclusion, the third definition is the best, but that does not imply that the statements made in the other three are wrong.

PROCEDURE OF A CONFERENCE

A conference, by definition, is an intelligently planned and conducted discussion with all conferees understanding and observing conference procedure. Although the discussion is informal, with a free interchange of question and answer or comment, it is nevertheless not a "gab fest." The presence of and participation by the conference leader tends to lend a quality of orderliness to the discussion. A description of the procedure of a conference is contained in the following paragraphs.

The conference leader opens the conference by stating the topic or problem for discussion. He then explains why this topic is pertinent to this group at this time. The leader may make some introductory remarks concerning the topic to prepare for the general discussion. If there is a need for a definition of terms to be used, this is also taken care of at this time.

When the preliminaries just mentioned have been finished, the leader states the first question and calls for replies from the group. The question may be directed to the group as a whole, or a certain person may be called upon. When the reply is given, the leader may ask for still other opinions. Each person is expected to take part with the greatest freedom and enthusiasm. It is not necessary to await being called on by the leader, but it is assumed that common-sense rules of courtesy prevail. Strict parliamentary procedure is never attempted. The more informal and spontaneous the discussion becomes within reasonable limits the better.

The discussion progresses from question to question, from subtopic to subtopic, under the observation and suggestion of the leader, who has prepared the questions in such form as to stimulate constructive thought in the required direction.

After the conference has proceeded until all the thinking and experience regarding the problem has been drawn out, the leader aids in summarizing and in reaching a conclusion. This conclusion or answer to the problem should be concurred in by the majority of the conferees.

TYPES OF CONFERENCES

At this point it should be stated that there are different types of conferences, and the different types have somewhat different uses. The different types and their uses are discussed in the following paragraphs.

Straight Conference. The straight conference, or, as it is often called, the open or unguided conference, is one in which the conference leader makes no effort to guide his conferees toward a predetermined conclusion. Even though he may disagree with the majority of his conferees regarding what constitutes a proper solution to the problem being discussed, he puts no pressure on them to yield to his point of view. As one member of the group he states his position and his reasons, but if his reasons do not appeal to the group and the group prefers a solution other than his, their majority opinion prevails. The leader has performed his full duty if he has drawn from the conference group their experience pertinent to the problem, has stimulated them to offer their best thinking to the problem, and has helped them to summarize their thinking into specific recommendations.

Guided Conference. The guided conference is one in which the conference leader attempts to lead his conferees toward a predetermined conclusion or line of thinking. The techniques used by the leader differ from those used in the open or unguided type of conference. In the guided conference the leader in most cases uses questions directed to named individuals, rather than questions directed to the group as a whole. The questions are so worded that it is difficult to give other than desired answers. The leader refuses to be sidetracked by questions asked of him or by answers not in line with his very specific questions. It is easily possible for an experienced leader to lead his conferees to a predetermined conclusion by confining the discussion to recognized facts and philosophies and by asking carefully prepared questions to which the wanted answer is practically the only answer. In doing this, he does not need to make any direct statements of his own. The sum total of the answers he has drawn from the group commits them to the conclusion and point of view that he had in mind before the conference began. And no one can truthfully claim that he has forced his opinions on the group.

This type of conference is useful in creating desirable attitudes in the minds of selected individuals, rather than in solving specific problems. It should be used only by an experienced leader, and even then with caution. Some individuals resent it, even though they admit the conclusions reached are in line with their own uncompelled answers. The reason for the resentment probably is that though such persons admit certain facts and truths, they do not wish to be governed by them. If the conference leader recognizes the presence in his group of a number of such persons, he should not conduct a guided conference with the group.

Case-problem Conference. The case-problem conference is the third and last type of conference to which attention is called. In this type an actual case problem is described to the group. It is usually a problem in human relations. It can be a local problem known to one or more of the group, or it can be a problem imported from some other organization. The leader fully describes the case as it actually happened, giving all the pertinent details. Then he asks the question, "What mistakes were made, and by whom?" The conferees in this type of conference usually participate with great interest, making a list of the mistakes and the names of the persons who made them. The leader's next question will probably be, "What common-sense rules of behavior and procedure can we formulate from a study of the mistakes made in this case?" This list comes readily and is recorded. In summarizing, the participants can make suitable recommendations affecting the group and the organization. This is a very useful type of conference, and is a welcome and helpful change after a few conferences devoted to technical or production problems.

Before concluding the descriptions of the types of conferences, it should be noted that the conference leader usually records the most important responses of the group as they are given. These responses may be recorded on a blackboard and later copied, or they may be recorded on large sheets of paper supported by a framework made for the purpose. This recorded material is then available for the preparation of a summary or report of the conference.

SIZE OF CONFERENCE GROUP

For effective discussion, a conference group usually includes no fewer than 8 to 10 persons, and not more than 16. The most desirable number is probably 12 to 14. A group of too few persons reduces the reservoir of experience and thinking power. A group of too many persons in a conference results in unequal participation, or, if each one is given his share of time and a full opportunity to speak, the available time may not be sufficient. Where there are 20 or more persons eligible for conference participation, it is in most cases better to divide them into two or more groups, giving each group its opportunity to discuss the same problem. The findings of the two or more conferences can then be combined.

If there are fewer than 8 persons eligible or able to discuss a problem and if it is an important problem, it is worth while to have a conference with the small number of persons involved.

THE CONFERENCE COMPARED TO THE LECTURE

A lecture is the presentation to a group of people of the thoughts, ideas, or opinions of the lecturer. The content or theme of the lecture originates with the lecturer (or a source back of him) and is presented to the audience, who are the listeners. The lecturer gives, the audience receives. In a conference, on the other hand, the conferees contribute the ideas, experience, and opinions, and the conference leader contributes only his pro-rata share while keeping the discussion on the topic and in other ways promoting an effective interchange of ideas. In some cases a lecture *may be followed by* a discussion or conference.

THE CONFERENCE COMPARED TO THE PANEL

In the panel a selected small group of three or more persons discusses a topic previously made known to them. Their discussion is under the guidance of a chairman and is staged before a larger group or audience. Usually each panel member knows in advance what he is going to say, but he may not know in advance what other panel members are going to say. In some cases, however, there is a rehearsal before the discussion is put on before the audience. It should be understood that in a panel discussion there is a preponderance of *prepared* discussion and only a little extemporaneous discussion. This method is useful in presenting to a large number of people the different aspects or points of view concerning a topic or problem.

In contrast to the panel, the conference has no audience, the conferees may not have prepared their statements previously, and they do not ordinarily follow a prearranged order in speaking. Furthermore, in a conference it is possible to have a cross fire of discussion that contributes greatly to the ultimate solution, while in a panel discussion this is possible only in a very limited way because the greater part of the program is prearranged.

THE CONFERENCE COMPARED TO THE CLASSROOM

In a conventional school class, the teacher presents material to the students. As in the lecture, the teacher gives, the class *receives*. The teacher actually presents ideas by telling, by reading, or by demonstration. Or, the teacher assigns tasks or experiments to be performed by the pupils, and these tasks or experiments are designed to provoke thought, growth of ideas, and realization of relationships or to perform some other necessary purpose. In such a class the pupil makes no contribution to the total sum of knowledge of the subject being learned. His efforts are directed to grasping what has already been prepared and furnished by someone else.

In the conference, on the other hand, each member or conferee contributes to the sum total of knowledge or information about a topic or problem. Each conferee's grasp of the problem is augmented by the contribution of the other members.

THE WHEN AND WHERE OF A CONFERENCE

Although it has been truthfully stated that the conference is an educational procedure, its method differs from the lecture, from the panel discussion, and from the conventional classroom methods. It is not a procedure to be used in all cases or with all groups. It has its disadvantages. However, it is agreed among those who have had experience that for certain groups and for certain problems it is the most effective procedure yet devised.

The conference procedure is best for a group of mature individuals of various ages and of approximately the same rank who have a common problem. For example, the conference procedure would be best for a group of executives of an industrial organization meeting to discuss a proposed plan of merit rating for their employees or to discuss changes in their seniority policy. The lecture method or classroom method is obviously not applicable. Nor do the men require a panel discussion, which involves a rehearsal of previously prepared material and requires an audience. Rather, they require a conference, which is just what the name implies, an intelligently planned and conducted extemporaneous discussion of a problem in need of an answer, a discussion participated in by persons greatly concerned with the problem.

The size of the group may affect the choice of whether there is to be a conference. If the group is too small, less than 8 or 10 persons, there may not be enough variety of opinion and experience to be stimulating or interesting. But if the problem is an important one, it will be worth while to discuss it even though only 2 or 3 persons are concerned. On the other hand, if the group is too large, over 16 in number, there is lack of opportunity for everyone to adequately take part.

Conferences usually are confined to the administration group in schools or other educational institutions. They are found in mercantile and manufacturing organizations, being used for personnel training and for problem solving. When properly used, they are of tremendous value.

CHAPTER 3

PHYSICAL ARRANGEMENTS

SIZE OF THE CONFERENCE ROOM

The conference room should be large enough to contain a conference table or tables around which chairs for 15 or 16 persons may be arranged. There should be room for an easel or stand to support the large sheets of paper used for recording data in the conference. Although the conference group is limited to no more than 15 discussion members and the conference leader, it is permissible to use a room large enough to accommodate 25 to 30 people, if there is such a room. A room larger than this often has acoustic problems, and in addition it makes a small group feel out of place.

SEATING ARRANGEMENT

The members of a conference group should be seated so that each one can look into the face of every other member. Not only can conversation be better heard in such an arrangement, but the facial expression of a speaker, which is often as revealing (or more so) than his words, can be seen. The chairs may be arranged around rectangular tables or circular tables. Sometimes the arrangement is V-shaped. To allow sufficient space for the easel that supports the conference tablets, it is placed near the leader at the more open end of the arrangement. It is important that the leader be able to see every discussion member and that all of them are able to see him and see the data that are recorded as the conference progresses.

PROVISIONS FOR COMFORT AND INFORMALITY

In order to work efficiently, men and women need to be comfortable. The chairs should be comfortable, but they should not be luxurious. Chairs with armrests are often used. There should be tables on which to rest one's arms, a notebook or an ash tray. There should be good heating, lighting, and ventilation. Smoking should be permitted if it causes no hazard.

FREEDOM FROM DISTURBANCES AND INTERRUPTIONS

Since the purpose of having a conference is to engage in serious discussion of a problem and through discussion to arrive at a solution, it is necessary to provide safeguards against interruptions or distractions. Therefore, the location chosen for the conference is important. The meeting place should be free from loud noises or other outside disturbance that may drown conversation or distract attention. It is better if there is no telephone connection in the meeting place. Following the same line of reasoning, all possible precautions should be taken to avoid having any of the conferees called from the conference room.

DEVICES AND IMPLEMENTS FOR RECORDING DATA

The best device for recording data in a conference is pads or tablets of paper whose dimensions are 24 by 36 inches or larger. Recording is done with a black crayon, not too soft and not too hard. The crayon should be soft enough to make easy reading 15 feet or more from the tablet, but it should not be so soft that it smudges and loses its point readily.

As pointed out previously, a blackboard and chalk may be used, but there is usually insufficient space on a blackboard for noting all that is to be recorded, unless what has first been set down is copied and then erased from the board. Then, too, white chalk is messy to use.

With the paper tablets, no erasing is necessary: when a sheet is full, it is turned back over the top of the easel, presenting a clean sheet for immediate use. If it becomes desirable to refer to something recorded earlier in a conference, it is easy to turn back the sheets and again display the data.

There are various ways of attaching the tablets to the easel. Usually a wood or metal strip is attached by bolts (with wing nuts) to the top of the easel, and the tablet top is clamped between the strip and the easel.

The top of the paper tablet (below the strip where recording begins) should not be more than 6 feet from the floor. If the tablet is placed higher, leaders of short stature find recording difficult and find it difficult to turn the used sheets back over the top of the easel.

The most desirable arrangement is three tablets, placed side by side on the easel. The reason for three tablets is to provide considerable surface for data that needs to be viewed simultaneously. This convenience pays for itself many times over in a series of conferences.

CHAPTER 4

CONFERENCE PROBLEMS

CLASSIFICATION OF CONFERENCE PROBLEMS

In a manufacturing organization, a list of problems and their classifications might be as follows:

1. Human-relations problems
   a. How can we properly select new employees?
   b. What training methods should we use to train present and new employees?
   c. How can we raise and maintain worker morale?
   d. How can we improve the handling of grievances?
   e. How can we get real teamwork from everyone in our organization?
2. Economic problems
   a. How should we choose a new factory site?
   b. How can we achieve a better distribution of our product?
3. Social problems
   a. What is the full responsibility of the company to the local community? How may these responsibilities be discharged?
   b. What steps should we take *now* and *later* to avoid racial friction in our employee organization?
4. Production problems
   a. How can we improve our production routing and scheduling procedures?
   b. How can we improve the handling of materials?
   c. How can we reduce waste of time and materials?
   d. How can we improve our maintenance program?
   e. To what extent should we use X ray in our quality-control program?

5. Policy problems
   a. Should we adopt some form of rating or measurement of workers in addition to quantity and quality of work, *e.g.*, dependability, versatility, etc.?
   b. What steps should we take to place promotions, demotions, transfers, and layoffs on a strictly merit basis?
   c. To what extent shall we use incentive wage payment on hard-to-measure jobs?
   d. Should we plan now for a change-over to an annual wage for our organization?
   e. What information not now being given to our employees should we give them? And by what medium?

The preceding problems are suggestive of many more that exist. It does not require a great deal of originality to add to the list.

In a school organization the following problems could be listed:

1. Is there a minimum amount of professional improvement *all* teachers should make every year of service? What should this minimum be?

2. How can we improve the behavior of students in halls and corridors when changing classes?

3. What can we administrators do to help our teachers?

4. How can we build up teacher morale?

5. How can we coordinate the educational phases of our schools, particularly to avoid duplication?

6. What constitutes the guidance duties of a classroom or a homeroom teacher?

7. How can faculty sponsors of school clubs and organizations do a more complete and efficient job?

8. Do we need better relations between teachers and administrators? If so, what can each do to improve these relations?

9. What can be done to get complete and accurate reports?

10. What are the causes of friction between pupils and teachers and how can they be avoided?

11. What are the causes of friction between the parents and the school and how can they be avoided?

12. What are the causes and the types of friction occurring between teachers and what can be done about them?

13. How can we interest our pupils in teaching careers?

14. What kind of a program can we develop to get teachers employed in business and industry during the summer vacations so that they can gain a better understanding and appreciation of life beyond the schoolroom which will benefit the pupils and which will help the teachers to respect their work as teachers.

15. How can we conserve pupil time so that it is possible to cover more ground thoroughly?

16. What are the pitfalls in a visual-education program and how can they be avoided?

17. How can we instill in, or teach, pupils a sense of responsibility?

18. How can we improve pupil attitudes?

19. What can teachers do to reduce tardiness?

20. What can teachers do to reduce absence?

21. How can we get parents to reassume responsibilities that they have forced on the schools?

22. What pupil attitudes need improvement and how can they be corrected?

23. How can we obtain more and better in-service teacher training?

24. Should teachers who have never taken courses in guidance be required to take them? Should guidance specialists be employed?

25. How can we promote better understanding and cooperation between general-education teachers and vocational-education teachers?

Nearly any school administrator can add many problems to the preceding list. He and his staff could profit by thinking their way through these and other problems.

SOURCES OF PROBLEMS

Any problem that confronts several people may serve as a conference problem. Usually such problems are those that affect members of the same group or organization. Although it might be possible, it would be difficult to find a worth-while conference topic that could be discussed satisfactorily by a teacher from a rural district in Tennessee, a minister from Boston, a lawyer from Philadelphia, a manufacturer from Cleveland, a farmer from Iowa, a miner from Pennsylvania, an orange grower from Florida, and a steelworker from Gary, with the conference being led by John L. Lewis. A group of rural Tennessee teachers could have a problem in curriculum construction; a group of ministers might have a vital problem of policy or of financing to solve; a group of industrialists might have a conference on any of a large number of pressing problems concerning employee training, merit rating, collective bargaining, etc. It is not difficult to find suitable conference topics from the list of problems confronting members of the same business or calling or in the same organization.

FACTORS GOVERNING CHOICE OF PROBLEMS

The two most important factors in selecting conference problems are

1. Number of persons involved directly and indirectly.
2. Relative size or importance of the problem.

Any real problem affecting two or more persons should be discussed. It is worth while to get agreement and peace of mind, for that problem at least. There is no rule to tell automatically *which* problem to discuss first. A problem affecting only two persons directly may, by remaining unsolved, affect their daily performance and so indirectly affect many other people. Such a problem would rate high on the conference program for these two. They should arrange a time mutually convenient and reason it out together.

There are other factors, such as timing, that influence choice of a problem. Because the timing is right, a problem often is discussed at an earlier or later time than originally planned. The timing may be related to growth of sentiment or to some incident that makes the discussion more pertinent at a particular time.

SINGLE PROBLEMS VS. A SERIES OF PROBLEMS

Usually there should be a planned program of a number of conferences involving problems of several kinds. A good program is a balanced program, with not too many of the same kind of problems following one after the other. In an industrial organization a conference program should contain problems from several classifications, one or two human-relations problems, several production problems, and some policy problems. Often one problem that is too big to be handled in one conference session should be broken down into parts or phases, and one part or phase should be discussed at each conference session. This makes for continuity of accomplishment. It also helps to prevent the incomplete treatment of conference problems.

Although various kinds of problems should be included in a conference program in order to provide rounded training, and to promote general all-round competency, it may be very desirable because of an emergency to insert a special problem in the series. The conference program should never be so rigid or inflexible that it is difficult to handle an emergency problem if one presents itself. The interruption should be taken in stride, and when the emergency problem has been discussed, the group can revert to the planned program.

CHAPTER 5

FIRST STEPS IN PREPARATION FOR A SPECIFIC CONFERENCE

WORDING THE CONFERENCE PROBLEM

Very few conferences are successful by accident. They are successful because of much careful preparation and planning. The wording of the conference problem has a great effect on the conference discussion, and for that reason it should receive the careful attention of the conference leader.

In wording a conference problem, the first principle to be observed is that a definite statement of the problem to be solved is much more challenging to a discussion group than is a general wording that is vague as to what the problem is or why it is a problem at all. An illustration of a general topic is "leadership." Much can be said about leadership, but many of the thoughts expressed may have little direct relationship to one another. If "leadership" is the conference topic (no problem is identified), probably no two of the discussion group will discuss it from the same point of view, and each person will have different reasons for discussing it. Many accurate statements can be made, but these statements will not necessarily make a pattern or lead to a conclusion helpful to any member of the discussion group. In other words, the talk is all around the topic and does not arrive at a destination.

On the other hand, if a problem centering around leadership is set up, such as "How can leadership be developed in an individual?" or "What are the 12 most important qualities of leadership?" or "How can we get foremen to realize the great importance of leadership in their relations with workers?" the members of the discussion group immediately have one and the same question to answer, one problem to solve. They have a place to go—a worthy objective for their discussion.

Another illustration of how to arrive at having a specific problem may be seen by considering the term "safety." A conference leader may be instructed to conduct a conference or a series of conferences on safety because "the plant needs to do something about safety." His preparation tells him that there is an organized safety program and what the weaknesses are, or perhaps his preparation may show that there is no organized program. In either case, his preparation is useful in the wording of his problem. If there is an organized program, he may use the wording, "How can we improve our safety program?" If there is no organized program, he may use the wording, "How should we organize an effective safety program for our plant?"

Presenting a problem is best accomplished by asking a direct question, as illustrated in the preceding paragraphs. Referring again to the topic of leadership, asking a question is better than using the wording, "Developing leadership in the individual," "The 12 most important qualities of leadership," or "The importance of leadership," although in each of these wordings the problem is implied. A direct question is a challenge, and its use in the wording of the problem is recommended.

The second principle to be understood in wording a conference problem is that most problems are parts of larger problems. Many problems are too large to be thoroughly discussed in one conference session. Therefore a subdivision or phase of the problem should be chosen for discussion in order that an adequate answer to that part or phase may be arrived at in the time available. If this part or phase is intimately related to other parts of a greater problem, these other parts or phases can be discussed in turn in other sessions. The answers to the various phases can then be coordinated to form the complete answer to a complicated problem. It is a mistake to try to solve a complicated problem in too short a time. Thinking must proceed logically, ideas, which form slowly in many cases, must have time to develop, and different points of view must come to a compromise through discussion. There is good reason then to word the problem in such a way that a part or phase of a complicated problem can be discussed adequately in one conference. If conference adjournment time arrives in the middle of a controversial point or before a conclusion is reached, it leaves a feeling of futility, dissatisfaction, and disappointment in the minds of the conference members.

The principle discussed in the preceding paragraph is illustrated by the problem, "How can we improve and permanently maintain the quality of our products?" This problem can be divided into several smaller problems, one of which might be, "What are the causes of poor quality of our products?" From the discussion of this one small problem, it might be concluded that some of the causes of poor quality are lack of adequate standards and specifications, lack of special training for inspectors, laxity in requiring standard procedures to be observed by workers, and lack of incentives not based solely on quantity of production. Merely identifying these causes and proving them is work enough for a conference of 1½ to 2 hours. It is impossible in one regular conference to devise remedies for all these faults. They can be discussed one at a time in some chosen order. Successive conferences could discuss "What do we need to do to provide adequate quality standards and specifications in our plant?" as well as questions based on the other causes of poor quality listed at the first conference.

PREPARATION OF DEFINITIONS

Many problems to be discussed in conference contain a word or phrase that presents a different mental picture to the various conference members. When this is true, it is wise to agree on a definition of the word or phrase so that all the group will be thinking and talking about the same thing. For instance, a typical conference problem could be "How can we improve the cooperation in our organization?" In this case "cooperation" needs to be defined. Some persons think of cooperation as being limited to response to a direct request. Others think of it only as refraining from knowingly hindering someone. Still others think of cooperation as being many sided, involving doing one's job the best he knows, going out of one's way to help someone who needs help, and knowing the other fellow's problem so that he can be aided intelligently when he needs it. Obviously a full definition is worthy of some of the discussion time in order that the members of the conference will have a common understanding as a basis for constructive thinking.

In his preparation the conference leader should be alert to words or terms that need definition, and he is justified in presenting definitions to the conference group. It is wise for the leader to invite discussion of them, rather than to insist that his definitions be accepted. If he has done a good job in forming the definitions, in most cases they will be little changed by discussion, and his work before the conference will have saved much conference time. The following definition of cooperation is usually accepted, and not much time is required in presenting it and obtaining acceptance:

Cooperation is the intelligently planned willing effort of individuals and/or groups of individuals working toward a common goal, with every individual or group willingly doing whatever is for the common good, even at the expense of personal or group inconvenience.

The short discussion of the definition brings out the significance of the terms "intelligently planned," "willing," "common goal," and "personal or group inconvenience."

PREPARATION OF THE OPENING STATEMENT

The leader's opening statement is for the purpose of justifying the discussion of *this problem* with *this group* at *this time.* It can be assumed that only real problems, not trivial ones, are important enough to justify taking the time of busy men, often high-ranking executives. It is equally obvious that the problem should concern the group called upon to discuss it. Their interest should stem from personal difficulties connected with the problem. In like manner, a problem is more interesting and discussion is more vigorous when the problem is a present or impending one. For these reasons, the leader needs to prove to his conference group that the problem is *real* and *big enough* to justify time for discussion, that the problem is *their* problem, and that *now* is the time for discussion. The leader should choose words that indicate his own awareness of the problem and he should provide himself with data to prove his statements, selecting data that are understandable to the conference group. The data may be from records maintained in various departments, such as the safety department, the personnel department, the inspection or quality control department, or the cost department. The leader should make it clear that failure to solve the problem will be costly to the conference members individually (in terms of "headaches," and perhaps through lowered wages) as well as to the organization as a whole.

The opening statement for a conference should be reasonably brief. In most cases from 3 to 5 minutes are sufficient. In unusual cases 10 minutes may be needed. The conference leader should not needlessly use discussion time. His job in the opening statement is to set the stage, to arouse interest and eagerness to get to work. Although the conference leader may know much about the problem, the opening statement is not to be used as an excuse to show off his knowledge. It should be used solely to prove the need for sound thinking by the conference group.

In summarizing, the principles to be observed in preparing an opening statement are (1) the importance of the problem, (2) the importance of the problem to the group, (3) its importance *now,* (4) use of factual data, (5) sincere, convincing language, and (6) reasonable brevity.

CONFERENCE MECHANICS

The first steps in preparation for a specific conference, which were discussed in the immediately preceding pages, may be called "conference mechanics." They are preparation steps that may be called standard steps to be taken in the preparation for any conference regardless of the problem. The use of these prescribed steps is responsible for the term "conference mechanics." Experience has shown that the use of these mechanics goes a long way toward insuring a successful conference. It is surprising and gratifying to observe how effectively student leaders can conduct conferences when these mechanics are used. These leaders obtain genuine conference discussion of a real problem and arrive at some reasonable suggested solutions that should be given a trial. And yet experience also has shown that conference mechanics can never be a substitute for sound thinking by the conference leader. Preparation that stops with the mechanics, instead of including an investigation of the problem, analysis of data, evaluation of data, and organization of ideas, is in reality permitting the success of the conference to rest *wholly* with the conferees, both with respect to their thinking and to their ability to organize their individual thinking into group thinking that is sound, realistic, and practicable. The right kind of thorough preparation by the leader does not result in his dictation of group thinking or of answers to the problem being discussed. It does tell him in what direction the thinking must progress; it tells him what are and what are not relevant data; and it provides him with some probable answers to questions he intends to ask. But all of this careful preparation cannot provide the leader with the experiences owned by his conferees and it cannot provide him with their own original thinking, both of which are so helpful and necessary for a workable solution to a problem affecting a number of persons. It should then be quite evident that conference mechanics alone or sound thinking alone is not enough for a successful conference. The best results are obtained when conference mechanics are understandingly used in combination with thorough preparation and deep thinking.

CHAPTER 6

PREPARATION OF CONFERENCE OBJECTIVES

THINKING THROUGH THE PROBLEM

It has already been pointed out that a successful conference is one that has been planned and prepared for. Some of the preparation involves identifying the problem, which has been previously discussed. After the problem is identified, the next step is to think through the problem. This often calls for abstract reasoning not necessarily related to the details of the problem as it now exists. This thinking through involves asking and answering such questions as, "Why is this a problem anywhere?" "What is the basic cause or combination of causes of this problem?" "To what extent is human nature involved in this problem?" "To what extent is modern science involved?" "What are the unique factors about the problem as it exists here?" etc. Again let us take an example.

The problem is, "How can we improve the morale of our foremen?" In thinking through this problem, the leader will realize that it is a problem anywhere because (1) it involves persons of different personalities and different training and different points of view who are required to associate and work together; (2) it involves an organization, which requires that some persons plan and give orders, while others receive the orders and do the work; (3) it involves the actions of individuals, which may be quite proper ones in a given situation, but which may be misunderstood by other persons. It is apparent that one need not know the details of the morale problem in a specific organization in order to realize that building and maintaining adequate morale for the various groups, or for the organization as a whole, can be a difficult problem to solve.

In thinking through a problem, a conference leader needs often to adopt the procedure of a doctor of medicine. The doctor notes the symptoms and then lists the causes that could produce the symptoms. A lasting cure must remove the causes. The conference leader, then, must search for the causes of his local problem, and for all the contributing factors, before he can determine the general outline of the solution—the outline that he will use in the conference.

SEARCHING FOR PROBLEM INFORMATION

After thinking of the problem in general terms, the conference leader progresses to the place where he is ready to consider the problem in its specific application. Logical questions to ask himself are "Who in this organization is familiar with this problem?" and "Are there any records pertaining to this problem?" These sources of information are investigated in the course of the preparation. In the problem, "How can we improve the morale of our foremen?" the leader should consult top management, foremen, and workers. He should investigate reasons for quits and for grievances, these often being a matter of record. All this preparation, thinking through, and search for information leads to the next logical preparation step, the selection of objectives for the conference.

THE SELECTION OF OBJECTIVES FOR THE CONFERENCE

The objectives are the subtopics or highway markers that lead to the final answer to the conference problem. Often the answer to the question, "What makes this problem?" gives the clue to one or more objectives. Again consider the morale problem. A logical step toward solving the problem is to uncover the causes of low morale. Therefore a practical first objective would be "To list the things that tear down morale in any organization." Logically, another practical objective would be "To list the things that tend to build morale in any organization." The objective that naturally follows is, "To identify the weaknesses of our own organization" (*i.e.*, select from the first list the things *we* are guilty of and from the second list those things *we* do not do or do not do well). Then the final objective is easily decided upon as follows: "To recommend corrective measures to be taken and by whom."

Another illustration of selection of objectives should be helpful. Consider the conference problem, "How can we bring our workers to have a keen personal interest in the quality of their work?" Thinking through this problem, a number of ideas come to mind. One of these concerns motives. We have motives for conscious actions, whether we realize it or not. Would a first objective for this conference be "To list the most compelling motives in the lives of average persons"? If so, a second objective could then be "To list the motives that would influence a person to do good-quality work." A third objective could be "To suggest ways and means of making these motives outweigh other motives in the minds of workers."

Another approach to the problem would be as follows: (objective 1) "To list the factors that contribute to worker indifference to quality work"; (objective 2) "To list the factors that would influence workers to do work of high quality"; (objective 3) "To study the two preceding lists as a guide in recommending specific measures to be taken to build up workers' personal interest in the quality of their work."

Either of these two approaches to the problem would lead to a profitable discussion. There are other lines of approach, but the examples given should illustrate the kind of thinking necessary in the selection of conference objectives.

There should not be too many objectives. Usually three or four are sufficient. If the individual objectives can be accomplished in a short time, there may be five or six. If there are too many objectives confronting a conference group as they prepare to discuss the problem, there is a danger that the problem will appear complicated and difficult, causing the conferees to feel discouraged in the very beginning.

The sequence of objectives should be such that the first objective is basic, a natural "first." The second should be a natural follow-through of the thinking, and the third a logical step following the second. Not all objectives present an obvious sequence. To see where they may lead, they must be studied by the leader. The sequence decided upon should be logical and defensible.

The objectives should not overlap or contradict one another. They must be reasonably possible of accomplishment by the group.

Importance of Proper Wording. The objectives should always start with an action word, or suggest action to be taken by the discussion group. Action words are more realistic and more challenging. Typical first words that fit great numbers of cases are

To list . . .	To formulate . . .
To record . . .	To recommend . . .
To identify . . .	To decide . . .

It is much more challenging to a conference group to see an objective that is worded, "*To list* the common everyday things that hinder teamwork," than to see a weak wording such as "Common everyday things that hinder teamwork." In this second wording there is no direct assignment of work to the conference group. It invites the thought that perhaps the leader will be good enough to supply the list ready-made and save the conferees the bother of thinking.

CHAPTER 7

PREPARATION OF THE DISCUSSION PLAN

THE OBJECTIVES AS THE BASIS OF THE DISCUSSION PLAN

If the objectives are well chosen and well worded, they are a ready-made guide to the discussion. They constitute a plainly marked highway down which the conferees can travel to their destination, which is the problem solution. The material presented in the preceding chapters illustrates this point. However, a problem and its objectives are presented to show the principle involved.

Problem: Should the organization adopt a new form to be used by production workers when on errands in departments other than their own?

Objectives:

1. To list the advantages if this form were adopted.
2. To list the cost of adopting and using this form.
3. To compare advantages with the cost.
4. To recommend for or against adoption.

Definition: The "new form" would be Form 158. It would provide space for the date and the name of the worker's department and would include a statement that employee (space for name) is on a legitimate errand (space for errand) in another department (space for department name). There would be a space also for the signature of the worker's department head or foreman. (These details are only suggestive.)

If a conference leader has the problem definitions (if needed) and objectives well prepared, and has presented an introductory statement that is convincing, there is no reason for delay in beginning work on the problem. The first objective invites discussion when stated properly. However, some conference leaders make a circuitous, indirect approach to the discussion. They make statements or ask questions whose relationship to the problem or first objective is not obvious. The group is at least temporarily mystified and, if the conference leader persists in this indirect and circuitous approach, the group grows more confused and/or impatient to get on with productive discussion. Unless something is done to bring the discussion back to the real and obvious problem, there will be no pertinent discussion, no real exchange of suggestions, experiences, and reasoning, and no workable solution. The conferees will come to the end of the session (conference?) dissatisfied with the result and, if new to conference procedure, doubtful of the worth-whileness of conferences.

To ensure a good conference, a good beginning represented by a real problem well prepared and well presented should be followed by a direct attack on the first phase or objective of the problem. From objective 1 the group proceeds to objective 2, and on through the remaining objectives to the conclusion. It is a businesslike, satisfying procedure. It provides a needed answer and gives the conferees a sense of satisfaction in a job well done.

LISTING TYPICAL OR EXPECTED ITEMS FOR EACH OBJECTIVE

In the handling of lists of items that may be developed under an objective, some may be historical or factual and thus not subject to much discussion. Other lists of items call for original thinking. It requires time to develop any list by discussion. To save conference time for the items that call for constructive thinking, the following device may be used. The conference leader furnishes a number of items of factual or historical nature, giving the group an opportunity to accept them and an opportunity to make possible additions to his list. The list is presented on the conference board for all to read. The kind of items that may be supplied by the conference leader is found in a conference on the problem, "Should we change our employee suggestion system?" Objective 1 probably would be to list the characteristics of the present plan. Objective 2 probably would be to propose changes in the plan. The leader could save much time in the discussion of objective 1 by listing the known characteristics of the plan as presently used.

With respect to items that call for constructive thinking, the leader will no doubt have in mind typical items or items that he hopes will be proposed by some member of the conference group. He should not list these, but should make a mental note of them. Many, if not all, of the items he has in mind will be offered by the group, and others the leader did not think of will be suggested. The leader will find it good practice to have as many items as possible on his list, but he should permit the conferees to mention them. If they are not mentioned and if the leader considers them important, he can bring them out by a conference leader's device.

PREPARATION OF LEADING QUESTIONS

The use of leading questions could be included in the techniques to be discussed later. But, because leading questions require preparation before the conference, they are discussed at this time.

To understand the importance of leading questions, it is necessary to understand the part played by the successful conference leader. The conference leader of necessity talks more than any other person in the conference. But he must guard against talking too much, against being too obviously or too frequently a teacher rather than a leader. He may recognize the need to do some teaching or to give some technical information that only he can give. At such times he should present and explain whatever is required.

For the few minutes involved he may function as a teacher who is explaining a problem to a class. The conference members may not realize the change from conference to classroom character, but the conference leader should know and be aware of the difference at all times. If he does not maintain this awareness, he is in danger of talking and telling more than his share as a conference leader. A conference leader should prefer that ideas be brought out by the conferees rather than be proposed by himself. He should think of himself as a thought stimulator rather than as a giver of ready-made ideas, realizing that he can develop the thinking of his conferees more by asking thought-provoking questions than by presenting an item or idea as his own. The leader should remember that people regard their own proposals and suggestions more highly than the ideas of others. If he can lead a conferee to say what the leader could have said in the beginning, the conferee regards it as his own and is more inclined to act upon it later on.

In his preparation for a conference, the leader should make some personal notes of items that probably will be offered under the various objectives or headings being used. He should especially note the important items, those he is anxious to have brought out without fail. Then, if they do not come out voluntarily in the conference, the leading-question technique is used. It is better to have prepared previously a series of leading questions for these important items than to rely upon the ability to phrase them extemporaneously. Some items are easily suggested by a question or two. Other items present considerable difficulty. A useful rule to follow in many, if not most, cases is to present a word picture of a situation in which the wanted item is a factor, but not to emphasize this item in the oral presentation. The presentation, however, gives a clue to the item. An example is offered to illustrate the use of leading questions.

Let us assume that a conference leader is conducting a conference on the problem, "How can we improve the individual and departmental teamwork in this organization?" and, in conjunction with his conferees, is building a list of practices that defeat or interfere with teamwork. The leader wishes to have included in the list the following practice, "Failure to promptly pass on needed information." No one has mentioned it, so he fishes for it by asking a series of questions such as "Why does the night shift complain that they don't know what goes on?" "What excuse is often given by the night shift when they do something they were not supposed to do?" "Why may the foreman of the shipping department fail to get out a special shipment that the sales department promised by telephone to a preferred customer?"

From one of these questions, or a similar one, will come the idea of "needed information that failed to arrive." The questions and discussion that bring this out will remind most of the conferees of many situations where this fault occurs. It is much better to have this important idea grow out of a discussion than to have it presented by the leader in his own words and accompanied by his own illustrations.

CHAPTER 8

TECHNIQUES AND ETIQUETTE OF A CONFERENCE

FUNDAMENTAL PRINCIPLE OF A CONFERENCE

It should be clear to the reader that a conference is a session where individuals pool their experience and thinking in order to solve a problem or to broaden the outlook of individuals so that they may perform their respective duties more effectively. The term "conference," as used in this text, means a session that is conducted by a leader trained in the skills required to draw from all the members of the group their respective experiences and thinking related to the problem or subject under discussion and to aid in summarizing the discussion into a form usable by the members of the group.

Since a successful conference requires that all members of the conference group speak their minds fully and frankly and since there are so many things that can prevent this full and frank discussion, the conference leader must be master of a number of techniques and must observe certain ethics.

CONFERENCE TECHNIQUES

Putting a Strange Group at Ease. One of the first techniques to be mastered by the conference leader is that of putting a strange group at ease. The group members or conferees may not know the leader and may not know one another. Before serious, effective discussions can begin, there must be a general feeling of friendliness between the conferees themselves and between the group and the conference leader.

To put the members of a group at ease with one another

and with a new leader, the leader himself must take the initiative. If he is new to the group, he should have the courtesy of an introduction by some person sponsoring the conference or series of conferences. Following the introduction, it is up to the conference leader. He should have learned composure so that he can speak without tenseness or strain. His first remarks should be those of genuinely friendly greeting, with some pleasant comments regarding the organization of which the group is a part. If his introduction has been brief, it is a good idea to impersonally mention some of his recent activities and to show how they provide a background for his work with the group.

If the leader finds that the members of the group are strange to one another, he should find some way of having each person's name and the kind of work he performs made known to the others. Small name cards including the individual's first name or nickname may be placed in front of each person. This helpful device may be continued until the leader and the group are mutually acquainted.

In putting a group at ease, the leader should never forget the usefulness of a sense of humor. An appropriate story or humorous comment can be very helpful in putting a group at ease as well as in making a favorable personal impression on the group with whom he is to work.

Treatment of the Too Willing Talker. One of the important conference techniques is that of preventing one or a few of the conference group from talking more than their share. No one preventive method is to be relied upon. If the leader has been asking questions of an overhead nature, *i.e.*, to the group rather than to a named individual, he may discover that one or a few conferees always respond before those of slower speech habits can get started. If not checked, this situation may continue through the conference and the following conferences. The situation requires tact, since it is easy to offend persons so that they cease to attend conferences or cease to participate in the discussion.

The leader may solve this problem by changing from

overhead questions to questions directed to named persons. Or he may be alert to cut in on the person who is talking more than his share. He does not make a rude head-on interruption, but cuts in at the first slight pause. His quick comment can be an agreement with the speaker, if it deserves agreement, or he can amiably ask the group if they agree. In other cases he may ask a named individual for an opinion, and then ask still another person to comment.

If the too willing talker continues to talk more than his share, the best method to help the situation is to talk to him privately. This has been done many times with very satisfactory results. He can be complimented on his interest and alertness. Following this, he can be asked how some apparently timid conferees, or those who are naturally more reticent, can be induced to talk more than they have been. By this question he will become aware of the need for everyone to enter the discussions, and he may suggest that he himself refrain from being the first to respond to a question or suggestion. Or the leader can tactfully suggest the same idea. Sometimes in this private talk the leader and the too willing contributor agree that the latter will himself call on one of the less talkative conferees, with a comment such as, "Bill should have some ideas about that," or "Harry, you had a problem like that not long ago. Tell us about it."

If none of the suggestions mentioned appeal to a leader, his own resourcefulness should supply a solution.

Treatment of the Timid Conferee. The problem of the too eager conferee has a companion problem in the timid or reticent conferee, who seems to prefer to listen and who participates in the discussion infrequently or not at all. There are many who participate too little. Experience has proved that a partial remedy for this problem is for the leader, in the first conference of a series, to present some data dealing with this condition. He may tell the conferees facts such as these: When a person attends a meeting and does not participate in discussion he will usually take away with him less than one-fifth of the helpful valuable information that is presented and may take away as little as one-twentieth, or even nothing at all. On the other hand, a person who participates in the discussion as much as possible or as much as etiquette permits, can take away most of the helpful information that is presented. Saying these and similar things to a conference group is usually effective.

During most conferences, however, the leader will find it necessary to make a definite effort to bring reticent conferees into the discussion. One method or technique is to ask direct questions of such individuals. In doing so, it is usually better to speak the person's name before stating the question. This gives the person warning to listen carefully to the question and gives him a few seconds to prepare his reply. The leader should be sure he is asking this infrequent contributor a question he can answer. If the conferee cannot answer it, he will be even more likely to maintain silence and let others do the talking.

As in the case of the too willing talker, the timid or reticent person can sometimes be helped by a private talk. He can be complimented for some good quality and encouraged to expose his thinking and experience. It can be explained that by so doing he will be helping to round out the general store of information regarding conference problems. Then, when he has made a contribution, it should be noted with reserved but sincere appreciation. The devices mentioned are only typical and obvious ones. To the alert and resourceful leader individual situations will present clues for other solutions to this problem.

Attitude toward Private Discussions. Many times during a conference several conferees may engage in a miniature conference of their own. Occasional exchanges of comment between conferees seated together are permissible. But if these exchanges continue for a period that distracts attention, they present another problem to the leader. He can stop the interruption by addressing a direct question to the person most responsible. Or he can maintain complete silence, looking meanwhile at the persons holding the private discussion. When this stopping of the conference causes the offending persons to pause, the leader can comment that perhaps the private discussion was good enough to be shared by the entire group. He need not say this with tongue in cheek. More than a few times this private discussion has been "on the beam" and is a definite contribution. If it is not "on the beam," the leader can good-naturedly proceed with the conference.

Recording. Because there is considerable recording to do when the conference is under way, the leader should learn to record accurately and with reasonable speed, and at the same time listen to any discussion that may be going on at the same time. If he cannot do this, he may miss completely some contribution that should be preserved. There are some leaders who not only can record what has been said, but can participate in further discussion. Most persons can learn to do this, but very few try it and persevere until it comes easily. It is a worth-while ability.

There is a point to be discussed with respect to recording items. Some leaders and some conferees like to have an outline list, with subitems under a major item, in order that any contribution that seems to be a part of a previously suggested item may be added at the correct place on the list. A technically correct list with respect to items and subitems (1, *a*, *b*, *c*, etc.) appeals to most persons after it is completed. Yet there are dangers in adhering to this plan in all cases. First, adequate space may not have been saved when an item was first suggested and recorded to make inclusion of a subitem easy. Placing the item in too small a space involves crowding, shortening, and possible distortion of meaning. Second, it may be controversial as to whether a certain subject is a subitem or another major item, and valuable conference time may be used in argument on that point. It is better to be liberal by permitting contributions to be recorded as new items. Relationships to former items, if they exist, can be identified by the conference leader when he prepares the conference report.

In building a list of items under a conference objective, it is not necessary to find and record every possible item. After a reasonable number has been listed, and especially if the time quota for this objective has been used, the leader should close the list. He can say, "This list is representative, and while it is not 100 per cent complete, it is sufficient for our objective. Let us proceed with the next objective." If one or two more items come out, however, he should accept them. The closing of a list should not be abrupt. The leader should not make an arbitrary stop that may offend someone, for it is always possible to come to a dignified and agreeable ending of a list.

While on the subject of recording, it should be said that recording itself is a technique. The leader may print or write. In either case he should be able to record legibly and with reasonable speed. The recording need not be beautiful, but neatness is desirable. Because time is a factor, the leader should take every reasonable opportunity to abbreviate. He may improvise his own abbreviations if they are not too strange or farfetched.

Finally, in recording the leader should be sure he records the real thought of the contributor. The leader may suggest a shorter wording, but should not distort the contributor's intended meaning.

Treatment of Cross-table Discussions. Sometimes there is a cross-table discussion involving several conferees that is pertinent to the problem. The conference leader should be alert to this situation and should immediately appraise it for importance and for probable duration. If he is standing and it appears that the cross-table discussion will continue for several minutes, he should be seated.

This provides an advantage a little later on. When the cross-table discussion has proceeded as far as is helpful, but seems likely to continue because of its own momentum or because of repetition of thoughts, he can quickly rise to his feet. Usually everyone will look at him, the persons talking will pause, and the leader can quickly resume leadership with appropriate comments. This technique saves needed discussion time.

Visual Aids. A discussion of conference techniques is not complete without reference to visual aids. Man learns more easily and quickly through his eyes than through his ears. Combining the two highways to the brain is still better. The author has noted that the presentation of visual materials has helped greatly in accomplishing the objective understanding of an idea by a conference group. For example, a cartoon showing two donkeys tied together vainly trying to individually reach two piles of hay, and then finally both donkeys eating each pile in succession, never failed to bring a laugh and to pave the way for a successful conference on how to make teamwork effective. The alert conference leader can find many visual-aid items to help him to put over an idea or to create an attitude of mind. In this connection, movie films are a definite asset. There are available some films, both silent and sound, that can be helpfully combined with a conference. The film should be presented before the discussion takes place in order that the discussion can clinch the idea or message treated in the film.

It is not practicable to attempt to discuss all the techniques a conference leader will need over a long period of time. There are many of them. An important one, the technique of asking leading questions, has been discussed previously. It is hoped that this discussion of the more important and most frequently used techniques will be helpful to the reader and student leader.

CONFERENCE ETIQUETTE

Etiquette is an important part of a conference. There are certain rules of etiquette that the leader should observe and certain rules that the conferees should observe.

Leader's Etiquette. The leader should be a gentleman at all times and should never lose emotional control of himself. There will be many times when he will be tempted to be sarcastic and rude and to abuse the leader's prerogatives. Since the leader is the one in charge of the conference, he has the authority to decide what is or is not pertinent to the discussion, to interrupt a conferee and request him to hold his remarks, to decide what is meant by the problem wording, and to decide how he shall record conference discussion. The wise conference leader, however, will never force an arbitrary decision on the conferees. He will always remember that his duty is to draw out experience and thinking from the conferees. If he had all the answers in the beginning, the conference would be unnecessary. The tactful conference leader will not "bawl out" a difficult conferee. He will let the attitude of other conferees be felt by the offender, or he will speak privately to the offender.

There is another very important rule of conference etiquette for the leader. Many conferences touch on or deal with delicate or explosive problems, where full and honest expression of opinion and of fact are necessary to a solution. Since few people will express themselves fully and frankly on such problems unless they are sure they will not be hurt by their comments, it is the responsibility of the conference leader to do all he can to protect the conferees in such situations. With this in mind, in many cases the conference leader protects the conferees by procuring from top management their assurance that no one will be censured because of the frankness of his statement, provided it is sincere and accurate. The leader may have a top management representative make this announcement to the conference group. In addition to these steps, the leader should make it clear that he will never link the name of a conferee to any controversial or candid statement. Finally, he can obtain the agreement of the group that individually they will adhere to that code.

Sometimes a conferee inadvertently commits a foolish

error in conduct or thinking. The tactful leader, to the extent of his ability, prevents ridicule from unfeeling persons and passes off the incident as lightly as possible.

Sometimes conferees ask questions that seem childish to experienced persons. But the leader should be quick to say that no sincere question asked for enlightenment is improper or out of order. This rule and those described above, fully adhered to, comprise the greater part of the etiquette to be observed by the conference leader.

Etiquette of the Conferees. The conferees owe one another courtesy and respect and participation in the problem discussion to the limit of their ability. No member who honestly tries to observe conference ethics will be rude to another member, interrupt him in mid-speech, or prevent the fellow member from having his turn at expressing an opinion.

Conference etiquette requires voice modulation to suit the conditions and avoidance of personal habits offensive to others. Before leaving the subject of etiquette, it should be said that the members of a conference group should observe meticulously the scheduled beginning time of the conference. Tardiness to a conference is not only irritating to the leader and to the members who have reported on time, but it is unfair as well. If the conference is delayed for the arrival of the tardy member or members, valuable time is wasted. If the conference begins on time and before the arrival of one or more members, their later arrival causes an interruption. Sometimes time must be spent on bringing them up to date regarding the conference up to the time of their arrival. In the great majority of cases this tardiness can be avoided.

SUMMARIZING THE CONFERENCE

Unless some good result occurs after a conference, the conference has probably been a waste of time. Although a work conference should be interesting, it is not entertainment.

The good that comes from a successful conference is the increased knowledge and understanding gained by the participants, the solution for a pressing problem, or a combination of these two results.

A conference lasting from 1 to 2 hours covers many points, proposals, and evidence pro and con regarding controversial points. Since agreements reached early in the conference are important and are just as much a part of the net results as are the later agreements, it is obvious that a summing up of the work of the conference must be made. This is the responsibility of the leader. He states the agreements reached regarding proposed action and how they were arrived at. He then calls for the final approval of the group.

In summing up a conference, the leader uses the data that have been progressively recorded during the conference. He should not use all of them, nor does he read them verbatim. Instead, he selects those items that are to be proposed or recommended for action to be taken, and summarizes them in his own words.

An illustration should be helpful. In a certain large organization a conference was held on the problem, "How can we reduce damage to railroad cars while they are on company property." The leader's summary at the end of the conference was as follows:

> In seeking an answer to the problem of how to reduce damage to railroad cars while they are on company property, we have listed the types of damage and the causes of such damage. From these two lists we proceeded to propose and discuss possible remedies. Some proposals we did not see fit to adopt, at least for the present. I do believe, however, that we as a group are prepared to approve finally the following recommended action:
>
> 1. Retrain our switching crews who move cars, and crane operators and other operators who handle equipment that may damage cars.
> 2. Closer supervision of these employees at work.
> 3. Purchase of adequate car-pulling devices which will eliminate moving cars by means of a crane.
> 4. Provide management with data to justify the purchase of special

cars for plant use, so that use of noncompany cars for certain moving can be eliminated. Special cars can be constructed so that damage will be greatly lessened.

5. Better track maintenance, reducing damage to cars that jump the tracks.

These suggestions have been discussed and are ready for final adoption. They will be helpful only to the extent they are conscientiously used. Each of you, representing important departments, has given tentative approval. Do you now give final approval to these five recommendations and do you now agree to put them into effect to the utmost of your ability? (Agreement was unanimous.)

Copies of the reports of this conference will be placed in your hands within 3 days. Other copies will be distributed to interested parties.

The summing up of a conference depends on the discussion objective as well as on the content. Some conferences are not so much problem solving as they are informative or educational. In summing up this latter type, the leader uses the same basic method employed in the summing up of a problem-solving conference. The recommended action, however, is more likely to be that of remaining alert to the new information and its uses, that of studying certain subjects, or that of discontinuing certain types of action. In all cases, a few recommendations are summarized and presented. The summary presentation should be enthusiastic and forceful (but not aggressively dictatorial) so as to make as certain as possible that the members of the conference group will do the things they have agreed to do. The conference leader as such has no authority to compel action. It is only by his persuasiveness that he can influence the conference group, and he is morally obligated to give as effective a boost as possible to the recommendations reached under his leadership.

PREPARING THE CONFERENCE REPORT

In a conference that involves the discussion of 8 to 15 persons over a period of 1 to 1½ hours, too much is said to be remembered by the individual members. Even if they could remember it, the discussion may need to be recorded as evidence and proof of agreements and recommendations. Persons other than those in the conference may be concerned with the conference problem, and reports are the best method of providing such persons with information regarding the conclusions reached in the conference.

The conference leader is the logical person to prepare the conference reports. He should do this as soon as possible after the conference is concluded, while the details of the conference are fresh in his mind. He is aided by the data recorded during the conference. The conference leader may prepare a longhand report, or he may dictate the report to a secretary. This latter practice is desirable, if it can be arranged.

The form of the conference reports may vary to suit the demands of the individual leader or to comply with the form preferred by the organization that employs the conference leader. A good and very practical form is recommended and presented as follows:

Problem
Objective
Definitions
Opening Statement
Discussion
Summary and Conclusion

In preparing a conference report, the leader should not merely present lists of items that may have been developed under the various objectives. Many of the items need a sentence or more of explanation. Wherever the item needs, or is improved by, an explanation or comment, this should be done. It puts "flesh on the bones," making the conference report much more readable and understandable, and therefore more effective.

The two typical conference reports that follow are presented as examples.

REPORT OF WORK CONFERENCE

Dec. 10, 1946

Problem: How can we improve the cooperation and the teamwork in the management-supervisory group in this organization?

Objectives:

1. To know what teamwork and cooperation really mean.
2. To identify those things that prevent or interfere with cooperation.
3. To identify those things that promote cooperation.
4. To recommend specific action that this organization should take.

Definition: "Teamwork" and "cooperation" are the willing coordinated efforts of persons or departments working towards a common end, with all persons and departments unselfishly working for the good of the cause rather than for their own personal ends. Teamwork often means that one inconveniences himself for the good of the team.

Opening Statement: When two people find themselves working together in a common cause, they have a problem of understanding one another and cooperating with one another so that they can work together efficiently. Whenever three people find themselves working together in a common cause, the same situation exists. The same is true for 10, 50, 100, or any number of people. This entire organization and every person in this organization should consider himself one of a team competing against other similar teams. The score is measured in this competition not in touchdowns, baskets, or runs but in the production of a quality product at a competitive price. The competing teams are other organizations making the same or similar products.

Visualize, if you can, all the employees of this organization lined up on one end of a tug-of-war cable, and on the other end a competing organization manufacturing the same or a similar product. The employees are supposed to be pulling on this cable in order to obtain as great a share of customer business as possible. If a photographer should without warning snap a picture of our team, how many would be shown to be pulling their best, how many would be shown to be pulling weakly and without much enthusiasm, and how many would be shown to be not pulling at all? The picture would undoubtedly show that there could be better effort at many places up and down the line.

You men know that parallels to this picture exist in most organizations. Your teamwork in our organization may be good, it may be above average, but it is not perfect. Somewhere along the line there is inefficiency and lack of teamwork. This is not always intentional and may be due to ignorance of what it takes to be cooperative. For this reason this discussion should pay dividends in outlining what destroys teamwork and, on the other hand, what builds it up.

Discussion: Discussion of the definition of "teamwork and cooperation" emphasized these facts: (1) Efforts to be cooperative must be willing and they must be coordinated. (2) There must be a common end or objective for the efforts of all persons. (3) Efforts must be unselfish. (4) One must be willing to be personally inconvenienced for the good of the team. (This discussion accomplished objective 1.)

Discussion of objective 2 brought out a list of those things that tend to hinder and defeat teamwork.

1. *A lack of consideration for the other person.* This means not realizing the inconvenience that we may cause another person, or not realizing whether or not he is able to do what is asked of him. In either case he feels irritated or frustrated, and desirable response is difficult.

2. *A don't-care attitude.* Many persons do not realize that they are paying the bill, at least in part, when they don't do their best. They think that the other fellow pays the bill and don't realize that inefficiency in manufacturing means added costs which the manufacturer includes in his

price and which working men the country over pay when they buy the product.

3. *A lack of planning.* There are many ways in which this can be illustrated. Failure to inform the other fellow is one example; failure to provide material and equipment is another.

4. *Poor instruction.* Poor instruction in some cases means "telling without showing." In other cases it means only one telling, which is never enough. A person cannot perform well if he has not been properly instructed.

5. *Jealousy.* Jealousy prompts a person to refrain from doing those things which he should do, or to do some things which he should not do, simply because he wants to "get even" with someone of whom he is jealous. Many people do these things because they don't understand the price of jealousy expressed in terms of poor teamwork.

6. *Unforeseen difficulties.* An example of this is machine breakdown, which in some cases might have been prevented by better maintenance.

7. *Failure to pass on needed information promptly.* Men in other departments or men on other shifts may need information you have in order to perform their jobs. If this information is too slow in coming, it interferes with getting the job done.

8. *Failure to give the "reason why."* It is human nature to want to know the reason back of things. It is complimentary to a person to give him that reason. People have brains to think with, and it is thoughtless and uncomplimentary to withold the reason whenever it is practicable to give it.

9. *Failure to ask advice.* An example of this is failure to ask advice of our equals or superior officer; an equally important mistake, however, is the failure to ask advice of one's workers. They are close to the job and very frequently can make valuable suggestions as to how to do work better.

10. *Failure to give credit where credit is due.* A person may have responded to one's request for a favor and thereby promoted the common interest, but it is just smart and plain common sense to thank him for it afterwards.

11. *Egotism.* A person who "high-hats" and lords it over his associates is a poor person to ask favors of his associates and to request cooperation from them.

12. *Asking the unfair or the impossible.* All of us are quick to react to requests that are unfair or impossible. We resent being asked to do exceptionally difficult, unpleasant, or unfair jobs. It is better to avoid such requests.

13. *Demanding rather than asking or suggesting.* We are living in a democracy. Military discipline in an organization is rapidly disappearing. The smart foreman or other executive will not make outright demands or give imperative orders, but will ask or suggest except in emergencies.

14. *Failure to understand human nature.* People differ in their motives and in their sense of values. The person in a given position can expect much more if he understands these differences in people and learns to allow for them.

15. *Poor placement.* People who are assigned to a job for which they are not adapted are usually dissatisfied and discouraged. A dissatisfied or discouraged person almost never does as much or as good work as he is capable of doing on a job which he likes and on which he can succeed.

The discussion of objective 3 resulted in a list of things that promote teamwork.

1. *Supply proper incentives to people to cooperate fully.* Not all incentives are financial. It was not developed in the conference, but for purposes of this report it can be stated that some may be promotional and some may be based upon commendation or citation for better than usual performance.

2. *Treat others as you would be treated.* In other words, follow the golden rule.

3. *Give adequate and clear and complete instructions.* Do not let the recipient go without being sure that he fully

understands what it is that is requested. This implies also that if instruction is needed, the recipient is given complete, adequate training.

4. *Give a person a "pat on the back" when he has done an unusually good job.* Commendation does not need to be overdone, but the tendency today is to neglect it. Let's tell people when they do a good job.

5. *Be cheerful and pleasant.* A pleasant expression and a cheery word is much more effective in getting results from one's workers.

6. *Accurate job placement.* Try to match people and jobs so that people are doing the things that they like to do and can do well.

7. *Be enthusiastic.* Don't admit defeat. Sell your program enthusiastically.

8. *Equalize the loads fairly among your workers.* Don't load some too heavily and others too lightly.

9. *Be efficient.* Getting things done with the least expenditure of time and energy, even under pressure, is an asset in giving and getting cooperation.

10. *Keep promises.* This is an excellent way to win friends and to give and receive cooperation.

11. *Be understanding.* If we are sympathetic with the other fellow's point of view, we will not make any unreasonable requests. Refraining from making unreasonable requests, coupled with the understanding of the other fellow's situation and point of view, convinces him that you are being considerate and prompts him to respond to your request if possible.

12. *Be impartial.* Being as ready to help one person as another in similar circumstances is an aid in winning cooperation.

13. *Plan accurately and adequately.* Good planning enables us oftentimes not only to do our work but to help out an associate in an emergency.

14. *Make helpful suggestions.* The ability and willingness to make helpful suggestions to others makes them your

friends and convinces them of your interest in their welfare. This sets the stage for needed cooperation.

15. *Do not be afraid to offer constructive criticism.* When complaints or criticisms have to be made, they should be made directly to the person involved. Of course, these complaints and criticisms should be constructive and should not involve personalities. Such straightforward man-to-man conversation creates understanding and respect and sets the stage for cooperation when it is needed.

16. *Be willing to work overtime or to suffer inconvenience for the other fellow.* Your help when he needs it is proof that you have his interest in mind and makes him all the more willing to render you a like service when necessary.

17. *Ask for and be willing to receive suggestions.* When one is faced with a problem, asking for suggestions from one's associates often produces the desired solution. It also compliments them, makes them feel some justified importance, and makes them all the more ready to cooperate.

18. *Be sympathetic.* A genuine show of sympathy when the other fellow is faced with a problem or emergency prompts him to respond with sympathy when you are in trouble, and this sympathy may take the form of active helping cooperation.

19. *Be forgiving.* If one is offended by another, whether intentionally or unintentionally, or if one's associates have little annoying faults, one should be forgiving and tolerant. None of us is perfect. If we expect to be forgiven and to have others put up with our mistakes, we should be equally generous.

Recommendations for the improvement of teamwork called for in objective 4 were suggested as follows:

1. Each person should take a personal inventory of his own actions judged on the basis of daily work with others. The two check lists contained in this report will serve as helpful guides in his analysis.

2. Within 90 days this group, with possibly others in at-

tendance, should hold another conference on this problem to measure results and to check further progress.

3. Other conferences should be held to inform more people regarding the value of teamwork and how to achieve it.

4. Seek and give constructive criticism within this group.

5. Take special pains to recognize the efforts of others in their performance of their tasks and in their efforts to work as good teammates.

6. This conference group recommends that management appoint a committee to consider how to improve work conditions in this factory. Improved working conditions tend to raise employee morale and are a definite factor in better teamwork.

Conclusion: A résumé of pertinent comments made during this conference follows:

In any organization cooperation begins at the top. Subordinates naturally look to their superior to set the example and the style. If the superior is cooperative, the subordinates will tend to be likewise. In general, if the superior is noncooperative and violates rules of teamwork, the members of the organization will do likewise.

There will be, of course, outstanding examples of individuals who will try to cooperate even without being shown a good example, but these persons will be so few in number that they will not make much impression upon the general run of performance. It is to the interest of senior management to follow closely the same rules of cooperation and teamwork that they expect junior management and their workers to follow. It is recommended that the senior management frequently read this report and check up on their own performance in the light of the advice given here.

The executive who fails to cooperate today is definitely hindering our effort. His lack of cooperation is little better than sabotage. Certainly noncooperation has the same result as has deliberate sabotage. Since end results are what count today, we can have no more patience with the noncooperator than we can with the person who deliberately blocks production. The executive (minor or top) who fails to cooperate draws the fire of all other executives in the organization. If he thinks he can go along as an isolationist in his own department, without regard to what other department executives are trying to accomplish, he is due for a rude awakening. It will not be long before other executives in the organization combine to treat him as he treats them. The noncooperative person soon finds that without the cooperation of others he himself is so badly handicapped that his results reflect only discredit upon him.

This helpful discussion will be of no value unless some concrete and specific action comes as a result of our discussion. This group reaffirmed its belief in the value of the recommendations made in the last discussion objective, and individually agree to take the action specified. The leader was authorized to take this conference report to top management for their study and to obtain from them approval of follow-up conferences on this problem and for the appointing of a committee to recommend improvement in working conditions.

____

Conference Leader

TRAINING CONFERENCE REPORT

Jan. 11, 1946

Problem: What can we do to decrease setup cost incurred in the manufacture of parts during substantial quantity runs?

Objectives:

1. To examine some factors that are responsible for excessive setup cost.
2. To determine which of the factors listed under objective 1 can be controlled or eliminated.
3. To outline steps for control or elimination.
4. To suggest machinery to be used to begin to put steps outlined in objective 3 into effect.

Definition: "Setup costs" are those incurred in getting a machine ready for production by installing proper dies or tools or by setting proper stops or gauges.

Opening Statement: Owing to the type of product manufactured at our works as well as to the types of machines necessary in this manufacture, the setting up of machines is quite a substantial item of cost. It is a well-known fact that the setup cost varies inversely with the quantity of pieces manufactured during a production run. For this reason, it is desirable to limit our discussion during this conference to excessive setup cost incurred during a substantial production run.

From the ditto forms which have been given to each of you, you will note that the setup efficiency on the three operations selected at random varies from 13 to 48 per cent. These setup efficiencies—or inefficiencies, as they probably should be regarded—are not exceptional, which emphasizes the fact that a real problem exists.

Further, you will note from the ditto form* that the broaches in the machine shop have been set up as many as four times per day for the same operation on the same piece part. In the opinion of your conference leader, this is an example of excessive setup cost.

The conditions under which our discussion will be held today are exceptionally good, owing to the presence of a rather large number of production foremen. There is no question but what you men who are in direct contact day after day with production problems are qualified to discuss almost any problem of a production nature.

The time consumed in our discussion of this topic problem could easily extend beyond 1½ or 2 hours; however, it is the suggestion of your conference leader that, in order to conserve time, the work involved in objectives 2, 3, and 4

* A copy of the ditto form passed out to the conferees for use during this conference is attached to this conference report. This form is a transcript from shop service cards, showing actual setup data for three operations on two parts.

be completed for each factor listed under objective 1 before going on to propose and list other possible factors.

In the write-up of the minutes of this conference, a copy of which will be supplied to each of you, this short-cut method will not be followed. The minutes will be written up in the order that the objectives now appear on our conference board.

Discussion: The first question asked by the leader was, "What factors are responsible for excessive setup cost?" The following factors were named:

1. Insufficient lead times.

   Comment: It was mentioned in connection with factor 1, that rush orders, as well as slow delivery and delivery of castings in small quantities, contributed substantially to higher setup cost.

2. No incentive is offered to operator for setup efficiency.
3. Lack of experienced setup operators.
4. Improper scheduling.
5. Failure to adhere to shop production schedule.
6. Improper routing of material or parts to the machines in the shop.

   Comment: It was pointed out that machines are often set up for each load of certain piece parts (especially going from drills to broaches), rather than waiting until a substantial quantity has accumulated.

It was also pointed out that the space alloted for banks in the shop is limited; however, it was the opinion of the machine-shop foreman that banking space is almost always available for a few loads of material going from one operation to the next.

7. Product devices not ready on time.
8. Breaking in of new dies.

   Comment: A minority opinion was expressed that this item of cost has been and will remain constant, and is not excessive.

9. Inaccuracy of standard setup hours on certain machines for certain jobs.

> *Comment:* Reference was made to blanket setup hours used on hammers, upsetting machines, etc., regardless of whether the dies are of a simple or complicated nature.

10. Improper charges of time on service cards to setup.

11. In the past, move cards written up in the production control department have not been rechecked before going into the shop for production of the item concerned.

> *Comment:* It was pointed out by the group that sometimes the sequence of operations of the unit on which an item is to be run has been changed by the time-study department during the period between the writing of a move card and the scheduling of the item to which the move card applies.

12. Lack of standardization of bolts and nuts used on various product devices.

13. Lack of a possible recheck of product devices before delivery to the production shop.

> *Comment:* It was mentioned by several members of the conference group that many instances could be recalled where the product devices delivered were not entirely in agreement with the product devices ordered.

The next question asked by the leader was, "Which of these factors can be controlled or eliminated?"

It was the feeling of the group that all the 13 items listed above could either be eliminated or controlled in some degree.

The next question asked by the leader was, "What steps can we suggest for the control or elimination of these factors of excessive setup cost?"

It was recommended by the leader, and accepted by all present, that the suggested steps for control or elimination of the 13 undesirable factors be considered in the same order as these factors were offered in response to question 1. The suggested steps are as follows:

1. Coordination by the production department and the sales department would go a long way to eliminate the evil of insufficient lead time. It was pointed out that certain progress has been made with respect to some of our products, and the idea was expressed that the same policy should be followed with respect to certain of our other products. If sufficient lead time is obtained from the customer by the sales department, it would allow more time for castings to accumulate, thereby increasing the number that could be machined per setup.

2. Keeping an efficiency record for setup similar to the record now being kept for production. It was the feeling of the group that such a record would furnish an incentive for the operator.

3. It was felt by the group that one of two systems must be followed in order to offset our lack of experienced setup operators. These systems are

a. Have setups made by special setup groups.
b. Give the operators skillful and intensive training on the job.

It was the consensus that item *b* would be more satisfactory for our plant, since the nature of our machines, as well as the limited number that require complicated setup, does not lend itself well to the use of special setup crews.

4. The factor of improper scheduling was felt to be a minor one; however, it was also felt that when instances of improper scheduling are noticed by the accounting department, these should be called immediately to the attention of the production control department. The opinion was strongly expressed by machine-shop foremen that in many cases pressure from a higher level of supervision is responsible for their machining smaller quantities of product than would justify a separate setup. In other words, very frequently production officials in levels of supervision higher

than unit foremen will not consent to waiting as much as 8 hours in order to gain the advantage of consolidation of machine setups. In some cases there is no question but what urgency of delivery is responsible for such irregularities; however, if sufficient lead time and skillful scheduling were properly coordinated, these irregular practices, which increase setup cost considerably, could be eliminated.

5. The disadvantage of breaking into the shop production schedule is well known, and it was pointed out that remedial measures are already being taken to eliminate this difficulty.

6. It was felt that in order to ensure proper routing of material or parts to machines in the shop, the unit foreman should be made directly responsible; however, it should be the duty of the accounting department to advise the production superintendent when flagrant instances of improper routing are noted.

7. It has been recognized for some time that a schedule for the product devices machine shop is needed in order to ensure a completion of product devices on time. This schedule is now in the process of formulation.

8. A regular scheduled trial run should be made for the breaking in of new dies in order to eliminate difficulties that are usually encountered at the time when the product is actually scheduled for production.

9. Blanket standard setup hours should be eliminated and setup hours should be expressed for each specific job. This procedure is necessary in order to maintain accurately the efficiency record mentioned under item 2 above. It was recognized that this additional time-study work might prove to be a rather long and expensive procedure. It was recommended that the time-study supervisor investigate this angle.

10. It was the feeling of the group that improper charges of time on service cards to setup would be almost 100 per cent eliminated if each job is given a standard setup time rather than a blanket setup time.

11. A system has recently been installed in the produc-

tion control department whereby move cards are rechecked just prior to their entering the shop. This system will help to eliminate any unnecessary moving of materials.

12. It was the opinion of the group that most of our lack of uniformity of nuts and bolts used in product devices is the result of retapping holders, etc., after threads have been stripped. This is a situation about which little can be done. However, it was also the opinion of the group that, wherever possible, close attention should be paid by the engineering department to maintain complete uniformity with respect to the original bolts and nuts used on the product devices.

13. The idea was expressed and given unanimous approval that all groups of product devices being delivered to the production shop should be rechecked before leaving the die shop or toolroom.

The last question asked by the leader was, "Who should be responsible to begin to put the remedial measures outlined immediately above into effect?" Again it was agreed to consider the 13 items numerically:

1. It is the responsibility of the sales department and the production department to provide sufficient lead time.

2. In order to carry an efficiency record for setup, the responsibility was placed on

a. The time-study department.
b. The accounting department.

3. The responsibility for training setup operators or providing special setup crews lies within the production department.

4. and 5. The responsibility for proper scheduling and adherence to production schedules lies with:

a. The production department
b. The production control department
c. The accounting department (accounting department to advise other departments when irregularities are noted)

6. Responsibility for proper routing to machines within the shop should be centered in the production superintendent, with the accounting department informing him when instances of improper routing are noted.

7. The responsibility for providing a satisfactory product device machine-shop schedule lies with the works engineer.

8. The scheduling of a trial run for a new die should be made by the production control department.

9. The provision of accurate standard setup hours for each job is the responsibility of the time-study department.

10. The improper charges of time on service cards will be eliminated with the fulfillment of item 9.

11. The responsibility for rechecking move cards for accuracy and current status rests entirely with the production control department. This rechecking system has already been installed.

12. The uniformity of the original nuts and bolts that are applied to product devices rests with the engineering department.

13. The responsibility for rechecking all product devices to be sure that the items being delivered correspond perfectly with the items ordered rests with the works engineering department.

Conclusion: The recommendations made during this conference to eliminate excessive setup cost have a direct bearing on practically all departments at our works. This is paramount to saying that any action taken must stem from senior management. All of the men present at this conference willingly pledged their cooperation in making the recommendations effective. This being the case, your conference leader, in addition to supplying a copy of the minutes of this conference to each member present, took a copy of these minutes to a member of senior management and urged that the recommendations offered by this group be adopted.*

* Senior management appreciated greatly the helpfulness of the conference group and cooperated in taking the initiative in making the recommendations effective.

CHAPTER 9

PLANNING FOR THE PROGRAM

THE JOB OF THE CONFERENCE-LEADER TRAINER

The conference-leader trainer faces a great responsibility and opportunity. He can, if he is competent, help individuals to acquire a valuable tool that can be used for the benefit of both themselves and the organization with which they are working. If he trains a number of capable conference leaders who regularly lead conferences, the trainer is reaching indirectly a great many people. Conference-leader training is not a job for a person who treats it lightly. Inadequate conference-leader training can be a liability to both the person himself and his organization. Poorly led conferences can be very disappointing; they can greatly retard the cause of industrial training and education of any kind.

The job of the conference-leader trainer is to teach, using the accepted steps in good instruction. He must present conference leadership through discussion and demonstration; he must provide opportunity for the students to try it; he must constructively analyze and comment on their efforts, and have them try it again; he must continue thus until the student leaders have learned reasonably well how to conduct work conferences and can proceed with normal follow-up instruction, which is also furnished by the trainer.

Sometimes the trainer is asked to help in the selection of the student leaders. Usually he is consulted regarding setting up the details of the training program. These things are discussed in the following pages.

SELECTING STUDENT LEADERS

Selection of student leaders should be done with a knowledge of the desirable qualifications of a capable conference leader. The more important qualifications are

1. At least average intelligence, preferably more than average.
2. Ability to think on his feet and under pressure.
3. Self-confidence in his own ability.
4. Ability to talk freely before a group.
5. Ability to reason logically and in the abstract.
6. Above average in oral and written expression of thoughts.
7. A well-balanced sense of humor.
8. Fairness and honesty.
9. Good character.
10. Neat appearance.

A conference leader needs to develop poise, which is greatly dependent on self-confidence. Therefore the conference leader must be sure he has developed, or can develop, competency in expression, an alert mind to keep up with other keen minds, and good judgment that will enable him to do the right thing at the right time.

In most cases the men who best qualify are college-trained. There are, however, some outstanding exceptions.

Actual selection is usually made by top management, on the basis of knowing the capabilities of the individual. Sometimes various tests are used, but at present this use is quite limited. There is no good reason why special tests could not be constructed and used with good results.

The observation of the author of this text is that the most successful leaders are between thirty and forty-five years of age. They have maturity and judgment in greater degree than a man in his early or middle twenties, and command more respect. The man above forty-five years will find it more difficult to learn to be a skilled conference leader. There are, and will continue to be, exceptions.

In a few cases foremen have been chosen to become conference leaders. This is a good practice. Foremen are closer to production workers than any other level of management, and foremen who are good conference leaders can put that ability to good use in conducting conferences with production workers. However, the percentage of foremen who can be trained to be capable conference leaders is smaller than that of many other groups. The greater number of successful leaders are usually superintendents, heads of industrial relations and personnel departments, safety directors, industrial engineers, and training directors. Most of these have had some college or university training.

ADAPTING THE PROGRAM TO THE NUMBER OF STUDENT LEADERS

The number of leaders to be trained affects the arrangements for the program. If there are 8 to 12 student leaders, they serve as a conference group while each one in turn conducts his practice conferences. This experience of serving as a conference member in the practice conferences of the other student leaders is a very valuable one. It furnishes a wealth of information and points of view on many problems. Every student leader trained by the author by this method has been enthusiastic regarding his experience. Some have called it a condensed college course.

If there are fewer than eight student leaders, it is recommended that enough other carefully selected persons be brought in to bring the number in each practice conference to 10 or 12. These additional persons are not to be trained as leaders, but are to serve as discussion members only. They may be changed as needed. The idea is to have enough persons present in each conference to provide a variety of experience and points of view.

CHOOSING THE RIGHT LOCATION FOR THE TRAINING

The training of conference leaders can be done on the employer's time and on the employer's property or it can be done in the public schools in the evening program. Since the employer who uses the trained leaders benefits from the training, it will be logical for the training to be done on the employer's property. The following considerations should be observed:

1. The room should be free from exposure to loud noises (such as passing trucks, trains, punch presses, etc.)
2. Lighting, heating, and ventilation should be good.
3. The acoustics should be reasonably good.
4. The room should have not more than 300 square feet of floor space, although larger rooms have been used.
5. The room should be equipped for conferences (equipment is discussed elsewhere in this text).
6. There should be easy and quick access to the room. However, the room should not have a telephone unless it is needed at times when conferences are not in session.

OUTLINE OF A PRACTICAL TRAINING PROGRAM

1. The trainer conducts a discussion with the trainees. This discussion includes conference leadership as a useful tool, comparisons of conferences and other types of meetings, techniques of a conference leader, and the preparation required for a conference. Opportunity is given for questions by the trainees.
2. The trainer conducts a demonstration conference with the trainees as participants, or a conference group is obtained and the trainees observe but take no part in the conference discussion.
3. The demonstration conference is discussed by trainer and trainees.
4. Each student leader chooses a problem which he will

prepare for a short conference* the following day (or as soon as his turn arrives).

> *Comment:* The student leaders are advised to choose real problems for their practice conferences. Actual problems in need of an answer help to make the practice conferences real. The advantages of this are very much worth while. In most cases not only do the student leaders gain experience in leading conferences, but, in addition, in the great majority of cases complete or partial solutions to the problems are obtained.

5. The student leaders in turn go through the first few steps of a conference.

a. Present a well-worded problem.
b. Present well-worded objectives.
c. Present well-worded definitions (if required).
d. Present an opening statement for the conference.
e. Conduct a discussion on the first objective.

6. The trainer makes a constructive analysis of the student's efforts.

7. The student leaders choose problems for full-length conferences.

> *Comment:* The usual practice for the first full-length conference is to use the uncompleted problem of the short conference.

8. Each of the student leaders conducts a full-length conference (usually 1¼ to 1½ hours). Each conference is followed by a clinic, which is the trainer's constructive analysis of the student's conference.

* The reason for a short conference is that there is usually some fear or misgiving at the prospect of leading a full-length conference. This misgiving is much less if the student leaders know that they must spend only a few minutes before the other students and the trainer. This short session "breaks the ice" and shows each one in turn that leading a conference can be just another important and very interesting kind of work.

9. Since conference leaders should prepare a report of conferences they lead, at this stage the student leaders are given instruction in preparing a conference report.

10. The trainer conducts a session wherein he presents additional information and instruction regarding conference leading. He has, in these first full-length conferences, observed some general tendencies that require discussion and offers advice concerning them.

> *Comment:* This session also provides opportunity for the students to ask a number of general questions that may have occurred to them, and it is sound practice to have such questions asked and answered.

11. The trainer conducts a second demonstration conference. By this time the student leaders wish to observe again how an experienced leader conducts a conference. Having had a practical introduction to the problems of leading a conference, they can appreciate the second demonstration even more than they appreciated the first one.

> *Comment:* The second demonstration conference should be discussed by the trainer and student leaders.

12. The student leaders conduct the second round of practice conferences, each one being followed by the trainer's clinical analysis.

13. The student leaders conduct the third round of practice conferences, each one being followed by the trainer's clinical analysis.

14. The trainer conducts a third demonstration conference. The first two have probably been of the free, open type. This third conference should illustrate another type, such as the guided conference or the case-problem type. (The different types of conferences are discussed in Chap. 2.) At the conclusion of this demonstration conference, it should be analyzed and fully discussed by trainer and student leaders.

Comment: It is excellent training for a student conference leader to be required to lead at least one guided conference. It requires him to think deeply and to be able to recognize those things that are basic in a problem, and to carry on logically from there. It gives valuable practice in phrasing questions that suggest a wanted answer.

15. The student leaders conduct the fourth round of practice conferences, each one being followed by the trainer's clinical analysis. The trainer again reviews conference reports prepared by student leaders, giving suggestions and help when and where needed.

16. At this time it is proper for the trainer and the top management of the organization for whom conference leaders are being trained to study the progress made by the student leaders. Many of the student leaders will be ready for assignment to work conferences. Others may need one or more further practice conferences before being ready for work conferences. The trainer should be available for follow-up and assistance to the new leaders as they continue to develop.

ARRANGING THE TRAINING SCHEDULE

A conference-leader training program can be an intensive full-time program, or it can be conducted on a part-time basis. There are advantages and disadvantages to both methods.

The Intensive Full-time Program. A full-time intensive program provides needed conference leaders in the very short time of 2 to 3 weeks, the program requiring 7 or 8 hours of work per day. If there is a quick decision to train leaders to meet an impending need, the training thus can be accomplished in a few weeks. In some instances, when production is at a seasonal low level, it may be that selected student leaders can be more readily spared from their regular work for a short full-time period than from their work part-time over a longer period when production is at or near capacity. Another reason for a short intensive program might be that the trainer would be available for only a short period of time. Summarizing, the most important advantage of an intensive full-time program is the short time involved.

The short-term intensive full-time program may have some disadvantages. Many executives are unwilling to spare selected student leaders for even a short time if it means full time away from their regular work. In such cases it may be difficult or impossible to find competent replacements while the student leader is attending the conference-leadership training program.

Another disadvantage is that few people have the capacity to adapt themselves to a daily drill of intensive mental activity, such as called for in group discussion, and to evenings of work in preparation for the next day's work. In many cases individuals who have been accustomed to constantly moving about or who have been accustomed to desk work that involves change or errands away from the desk have suffered headaches or extreme mental fatigue as a result of the 7 or 8 hours each day of conference discussion and of the hours spent in outside preparation. Sometimes the adjustment to this intensive work is not made until near the close of the program.

In the minds of most persons, new ideas need time to "jell." In an intensive full-time program new facts and ideas of all kinds come too rapidly to be assimilated by the average person. After a day or two his mind becomes congested with new ideas not fully comprehended and not properly put away for future use. Until this mental congestion disappears, new ideas cannot receive proper attention. A skilled trainer can help this situation by advice and comments, by creating an atmosphere of relaxation while at work, by intermissions between conferences, and by other means to be thought of by a resourceful trainer aware of the conditions existing at the time. But he cannot do more than prevent a small part of this confusion and fatigue. The intensive program is best suited to those individuals whose normal workday is one of meeting new situations and taking part in discussions that require quick and incisive thinking.

The Part-time Program. A part-time program extending over 6 to 10 weeks appeals to many executives and to many students of conference leadership. This program can be 1 day each week for as many weeks as are necessary, the number of weeks depending upon the number of leaders to be trained. In some cases it has been advantageous to use 2 days per week. This arrangement has been used by a number of organizations and has worked out very well.

The advantages of the part-time program are probably obvious after reading the preceding paragraphs. Briefly stated, they are the minimum interference with regular duties of the student leaders and the easier adjustments of individuals to learning new skills and to the discussion of many problems, problems of which they may have been aware but have not had opportunity and need to discuss. In the part-time program new problems and new ideas do not come too rapidly for assimilation by the average student leader.

The most important disadvantage (but fortunately one that seldom needs to be faced) is that of a long training period in the face of an immediate need.

The selection of the day or days for a part-time program must be made with reference to the days most suitable to the organization, the student leaders, and the trainer. One good thought to keep in mind is that the first and middle parts of the week are much better than the last days, namely, Friday and Saturday. Usually there are tasks that must be finished before the work week ends, and a temporary program will be more agreeable to all concerned if it does not interfere with these week-end tasks.

With respect to hours of the day for the part-time program, it is better to permit the students to have one-half to three-quarters of an hour at the beginning of the day to give instructions to subordinates, receive reports, etc., before the training program starts. There should be a minimum of 3½ hours for the program in the forenoon, including a 5-minute intermission. During the lunch hour a student leader may possibly have time for a look at an item that he is following closely. The afternoon session should provide another minimum of 3½ hours of work. Following this session, the trainer usually spends some time with one or more of the student leaders, answering questions or helping in the preparation for a conference. Frequently there is an evening session to supplement the day sessions. These are useful for demonstration conferences conducted by the trainer or for trouble-shooting sessions, where the students ask questions for the trainer to answer or the trainer comments on faults or tendencies he has observed.

In scheduling the short full-time intensive program, there is little difficulty regarding choice of days, since the program runs at least 5 days per week, and it may run 5½ days. The hours of the day to be given to the program are usually determined by what time is convenient for the leader and the students. There should be a minimum of 7 hours of work, plus some preparation in the evenings by the student leaders.

CHAPTER 10

CONDUCTING THE PROGRAM

INTRODUCTORY SESSION

In training conference leaders, it has been tested and proved over a long period of time that an introductory session is the best way to commence the program. The first part of such a session is used to outline the procedures and sequence of the entire program. This outline is helpful and useful in giving the student leaders a picture of what is in store.

The second part of the introductory session is used to review briefly the course outline. Text materials are furnished each student. It is preferable to furnish these materials to the students a day or two before the program begins in order to provide opportunity for the text to be read before the first, or introductory, session. In the first session the trainer reviews each unit, not reading the text, but presenting the ideas treated in the text and commenting on them. His oral presentation should use examples and illustrations to supplement the text. There are questions by the students, and these are answered by the trainer. If the session is well conducted, it is of tremendous interest and value to the student leaders. It leaves them enthusiastic and eager for what is to follow.

It seems appropriate at this point to state that the training of conference leaders, as presented in this text, conforms to proved training techniques. The four principle steps used and publicized in recent years are *tell* the student; *show* the student; have the *student try it; check, correct,* and *follow up.* The first session conducted by the trainer is part of step 1. The demonstration conferences are parts of step 2. The students' practice conferences are step 3. The clinics and individual help by the trainer, and his follow-up, are step 4.

THE TRAINER'S DEMONSTRATION CONFERENCES

The demonstration conferences led by the trainer are of great importance. There are two methods that may be used. The trainer may use his student leaders as the conference discussion group, or he may arrange for a special discussion group, and lead a conference wherein the student leaders are observers and not participants. Both methods have advantages and disadvantages.

With respect to the first method, the students often pay most or all their attention to the conference problem and its solution, and very little attention to conference-leadership techniques. In this connection, the trainer should not interrupt his conference to draw attention to the various techniques. These techniques should not in most cases be obvious, particularly to the conference participants. It is easy for persons with no experience in conference leadership to miss or fail to recognize many of the devices and techniques used by the experienced leader. In the case of student leaders, this disadvantage can be partly compensated for by explanations by the trainer in the discussion period that follows his demonstration conference. The conference is fresh in their minds, and the trainer can remind the students of a certain place in the discussion when he did this or that, and he can give his reasons for so doing. Most of the students will remember the place indicated and can then understand the point the leader is seeking to emphasize.

In the second method that may be used for a demonstration conference, the student leaders, because they are observers and not participants, not only follow the discussion with interest, but they probably will be much more aware of the techniques used by the trainer who is leading the demonstration conference. There will still be some temptation for the students to be concerned with the problem solution. It is to be remembered that demonstration conferences and practice conferences should deal with real problems that are of interest to everyone.

A disadvantage of the latter method, in most cases slight, is that some individuals in a discussion group are affected by the presence of observers. They do not enter into discussion as freely and frankly as they would if there were no observers. The trainer can help prevent this disadvantage by explaining casually before the discussion begins that the student observers are not interested in the content of the individual contributions so much as in the over-all aspects of the conference and in the methods used to reach a solution to the problem.

As in the case of the demonstration conference where the students are the discussion group, the demonstration conference where the students are observers is followed by a clinic, or discussion of the conference. These clinics are of value in that the trainer can relate actual performance to points covered in the introductory session, where conference-leadership text materials were being studied.

ARRANGING PROBLEMS FOR STUDENT LEADERS' CONFERENCES

With a group of 8 to 10 student leaders, each of whom should lead at least four full-length practice conferences, there are from 32 to 40 conferences for which real problems need to be provided. This may seem to be a very difficult task. Where can that many real problems be found? Actually it is not difficult. Chapter 4 in the course outline and the corresponding information sheets go far toward answering that question. In addition, following is a list of problems that have been used in various conference-leader training programs.

1. Should this organization adopt a policy of providing written descriptions of all supervisory and administrative jobs?

2. What shall we recommend to top management regarding written descriptions of supervisory jobs?

3. What can we do to have employees in this plant properly and satisfactorily carry out their instructions?

4. How can we improve the keeping of necessary records, both departmental and consolidated?

5. What can foremen do to cooperate more effectively with the industrial engineering department in order to improve job methods?

6. To what extent can we use group training in this plant?

7. What are the most effective methods for group training?

8. What can foremen do to reduce the waste of time by their workers?

9. What is the relationship between administration and supervision?

10. How can we improve our new-employee induction program?

11. How can we reduce the too high costs in our molding department?

12. What can we do to improve our safety program?

13. Considering our product and its use by our customers, is it good enough, or should we improve the quality?

14. How can we improve movement of materials *to* and *in* the foundry?

15. How can we increase our employees' job interest?

16. To what extent should we use X ray in our quality control?

17. How can we improve the housekeeping in our plant?

18. To what extent should apprentice training be used in this works?

19. How can we reduce absenteeism?

20. How can we improve our suggestion system?

21. What shall we recommend as the principles of a fair promotion, demotion, and layoff policy?

22. How can we do a better job of training new clerical workers?

23. To what extent can we use welding in the fabrication of our product?

24. Should we provide cafeteria service in this works?

25. Should we install a merit-rating system in this plant?

It would not be difficult to record one hundred or more good conference problems. However, the list provided should be sufficiently suggestive that local problems can be uncovered without difficulty. One training director frequently asks his associates what their "headaches" are. He receives some very realistic replies, eloquently stated. From these replies he obtains needed work for his conference groups and for special training groups.

It is good practice to have the student leaders choose their own problems for their practice conferences. Helpful suggestions can be made, but seldom should a problem be handed to a student. Willing interested student leaders usually prefer problems of their own choosing. Usually, too, students will choose problems concerning which they have knowledge or interest, or both, and these are an asset in preparation for the conference.

HELPING STUDENT LEADERS PREPARE FOR A CONFERENCE

It is often necessary for the trainer to help the individual student leaders with their preparation. Their problem may not be well phrased, and the objectives may not be adequate, well phrased, or in proper sequence. Needed definitions may be lacking, definitions may be supplied for terms that need no definition, or the definitions given may be faulty.

There may be many mistakes or shortcomings that will be evident in the student leader's preparation. It is to his advantage to have them pointed out to him by a competent trainer. It is no kindness to the student leader to let mistakes and shortcomings pass without comment. The student leader wishes to become an excellent leader, and his superior officers in the organization, having selected him for training, wish that training to be the best so that their investment in him will pay dividends. A conscientious trainer will earnestly wish his students to become excellent leaders. Therefore he will do everything he can to be sure the preparation for practice conferences is good. Very seldom will the quality of a conference be better than the preparation. This happens only when the excellence of the contributions of the conference group outweighs the inadequate preparation of the leader. If possible, the trainer should schedule the student leaders for individual help on their coming practice conference. He owes them a good start, and if it is within his authority or privilege to give them freely of his time and experience, he should by all means do so.

THE CONFERENCE ANALYSIS, OR CLINIC

During the practice conferences the trainer should not make it a regular practice to participate in the discussion. He should be seated back of the group around the conference table, but in a location where he can see and hear the conference in progress. Unless it is a very special point of procedure, the trainer permits the student leader to proceed "on his own" through the complete conference. It is not conducive to good discussions to interrupt the student leader and the group in order to make a correction. To do this would needlessly embarrass the student leader and throw the discussion out of stride. There is a much better way, and that is by means of the clinic, or conference-analysis session, that follows the practice conference.

In preparation for the clinic, and for the convenience of the trainer, a student conference-leader rating form is recommended.* While the practice conference is in progress,

* The student-leader rating form is presented on pp. 84-87.

the trainer observes and makes appropriate notations on the rating form. This form is planned to require a minimum of writing, yet there is space for specific comments if the trainer wishes to record them. After the practice conference is finished, the clinic follows immediately, and the trainer uses the rating form as the basis for his comments.

The clinic for each practice conference is conducted before all the student leaders, rather than privately with the student who conducted the conference. It is helpful to all the student leaders to hear constructive suggestions regarding each practice conference in which they participate. They may have ideas regarding how well the other students conducted their conferences, and it is helpful for them to compare their own ideas with those of the trainer. There is no censure if a student leader makes a mistake. The trainer analyzes that part of the conference where the mistake (or weakness) occurred, and suggests how it could be improved.

Although the trainer should be kind and tactful, he should not intentionally overlook weaknesses in the performance of the student leaders. Nor should he permit them to believe that they have given a better performance than is actually the case. That would not be fair or wise, considering their later work conferences for which they should have the best and most thorough preparation and training. A too softhearted trainer, or one who mistrusts his own tactfulness and permits student shortcomings to go unmentioned and uncorrected, can be responsible for great injustice to his students and responsible for lack of success of the program in which the student leader is later to have a prominent part.

There is need for the trainer to encourage student leaders who underestimate their performance and ability. Many student leaders are too critical of themselves, particularly in the first one or two practice conferences. The leader knows whether they are underrating their efforts and, in such a case, should encourage them with the facts that only he can give.

It should be explained to student conference leaders that in a given conference a leader may make many errors and break many rules of conference leadership and still have a successful conference. On the other hand, a leader may conduct a technically near-perfect conference and accomplish little or nothing. One of the criteria by which the success of a conference is judged is the character of the conclusions reached. The controlling factors in these cases are the discussion members. In the case of a conference that is successful in spite of poor leadership, the discussion members carry the load, are informed and cooperative, and the conference ends with practical and worth-while conclusions. In the case of a conference that is unsuccessful in spite of technically perfect leadership, the discussion members may not be informed or they may not be cooperative, and no worth-while conclusions result.

The well-conducted clinic is not a lecture or a one-way discussion by the trainer. He should draw out questions from the student leaders if none come on their initiative. If the leader has established the proper cordial, friendly work relations with his student leaders and if he explains the various steps of the program as he should, questions in the clinic will come voluntarily. He should often use the technique of asking the student leader why he did a certain thing, before implying that it was improper. The student leader may have had a good reason, and this may change the trainer's point of view and his comments.

In the clinics following the first two or three rounds of practice conferences, the trainer should not ask the student leaders for their own opinions regarding the practice conference conducted by one of their members. It would be improper to ask for constructive analysis by students who are just making a start in learning how to lead conferences. Conference leading is not so simple and easy that novices can make a competent analysis of a conference. However, after well-selected student leaders have conducted two or three conferences and have participated as discussion members in 25 to 30 other conferences, they can be expected to have learned many things concerning conference leadership and to be able to make competent analyses.

When the student leaders have developed some competence in analysis, it is good practice for the trainer to ask the student leaders for their opinions of one another's conference and for constructive suggestions. It is worth while for the trainer to know whether or not his analyses are in accord with the thinking of his students. If a majority of his students should disagree with him in a number of cases, he should reexamine his own analysis with care. Should he come to the conclusion that they are equally correct, or more nearly correct than he, he should quickly and sincerely acknowledge it. If his student leaders as a group react in a certain way to a given leader's conduct of a conference, it is very probable that other groups would react in the same way to the same kind of leadership.

The possible differences of opinion between the trainer and his student leaders concerning the conduct of the conference are few and for that reason are not a cause for concern. The greatest value derived from inviting student leaders to assist in the analysis of another leader's conduct of a conference is the development of their alertness to conference-leadership techniques.

Rating Form for Student Conference Leaders

Problem: Check appropriate descriptive phrase.

Well stated, meaning clear ________. Contained one word, phrase, or idea that was not clear, but permitted conferees to be reasonably sure of meaning ________. Not clear, resulting in considerable doubt ________.

Comments: ____

____

____

Objectives: Check appropriate descriptive phrase.

Expressed action rather than asked a question _______. All clearly stated _______. One or more not clear _______. In logical sequence _______. Reasonably attainable _______. Attainment doubtful _______. Objectives listed are sufficient to fully solve the problem _______. Not sufficient _______.

Comments: ____

____

____

Definitions: Check appropriate descriptive phrase.

None needed _______. Needed, adequately supplied _______. Partly supplied, adequate as far as given, needed more _______. Supplied, but unsatisfactory _______.

Comments: ____

____

____

Opening Statement: Check appropriate descriptive phrase.

Challenging, well delivered, aroused desire to do something about the problem _______. Interesting, challenging content, lacked punch in delivery_______. Mediocre content as to interest, weak delivery _______.

Comments: ____

____

____

Discussion: Check appropriate descriptive phrase.

What was the over-all character of this session? Did it have the atmosphere of a conference _______. If not, what was it _______

____

____

Questions were clear, well phrased _______. Questions were logical, pertinent to objective _______. Questions were confusing _______. The leader was able to ask questions that brought out points he had in mind but did not wish to offer personally _______. The leader promoted cross-table discussion _______.

Comments: ____

____

____

Recording: Check appropriate descriptive phrase.

Recording was reasonably fast _______. Recording was too slow _______. Recording was reasonably legible and neat _______. Recording was legible but not neat _______. Used abbreviations well _______. Did not abbreviate _______. Abbreviated awkwardly _______. Recorded the real meaning of the contributions. Failed to record the real meaning of the contributions to the conferees _______. Leader answered too many questions _______. Failed to recognize a contribution _______. Recording a heading for every list of items _______.

Comments: ____

____

____

Over-all Character of the Conference: Check appropriate descriptive phrase.

Leader refrained from imposing his opinions _______. Leader often seemed to impose his opinions _______. Leader turned back questions to the conferees _______. Leader answered too many questions _______.

Comments: ____

____

____

Leader obtained considerable contribution from every conferee _______. Missed one or more entirely _______. Permitted one or more to take too little part _______. Leader permitted one or more conferees to monopolize the discussion _______.

Comments: ____

____

____

Leader was properly aggressive _______. Leader was too aggressive _______. Leader was insufficiently aggressive _______.

Comments: ____

____

____

Leader's thinking was adequately fast ______. Leader's thinking was too slow ______. Leader not only grasps the meaning of contribution, but reads between the lines to foresee the next step in the reasoning or grasps the personal reason for a comment ______.

Comments: ____

____

____

Leader planned and successfully followed a timetable for conference progress ______. Leader apparently failed to have or follow a timetable (too much time for one or more objectives, too little for others) ______. Leader failed to estimate within reasonable limits the time required for the various objectives: Not enough ______. Too much ______.

Comments: ____

____

____

Conclusion: Check appropriate descriptive phrase.

Leader summarized tellingly, clearly, and caused machinery for action to be set up ______. Leader summarized tellingly, clearly, let action rest with the conferees ______. Leader summarized clearly, but not tellingly, let action rest with conferees ______. Leader's summary definitely weak, called for no action ______.

Comments: ____

____

____

DEFINITIONS AND EXPLANATIONS OF ITEMS IN THE RATING FORM

For the most part, the items are understandable to the reader without definition or explanation. Yet there are some items that need elaboration and these are explained here. The discussion should aid the reader in a better understanding and appreciation of the rating form.

Problem. A problem that is well stated and clear in meaning is one that carries one and the same clearly defined meaning in the minds of all of the conferees. An example of a well-stated problem presented for discussion by a group of school principals follows:

What can we do to offer practical aid to our teachers? An example of a problem statement that contained one word or phrase that was not clear, but permitted the conferees to be reasonably sure of the meaning is

What can we as administrators do to offer practical aid to our teachers? The second of the two examples was actually used and was directly responsible for using 20 minutes of conference time to finally agree that "we as administrators" and "we" meant exactly the same group of people. (The conference group was composed of school principals and one superintendent.)

Objectives. "Expresses action" means to begin with a verb form, such as "to list," "to analyze," "to recommend," etc.

By "attainable" is meant in the time available for the conference.

By "objectives sufficient to solve the problem" is meant that the sum total of work required by the objectives results in definite solutions to the problem as stated. Without adequate, clearly stated objectives, a number of suggestions could be made without group recommendation to use one or more as an actual solution to a problem demanding a recommended solution. Or, a solution could be recommended, but with no indication of how or by whom it was to be carried out.

Opening Statement. The opening statement should indicate the reason why this problem is presented for discussion at this time and before this group. Proof of the importance of the problem should be offered, using concrete data such as statistics and illustrations. In rating the opening statement, the amount of proof of the existence of the problem should be considered first, and then the skill and effectiveness of the presentation. Did the opening statement leave the participants "cold," eager to solve the problem, or what degree between the two extremes?

The Over-all Character of the Conference. The atmosphere of a conference should be that of general participation, an orderly, friendly exchange of ideas quietly guided, but not repressed or dictated, by the leader. It would be more like a lecture if the leader monopolized the discussion and was continually offering his own ideas.

Aggressiveness. By "aggressiveness" is meant the willingness and *ability* of the conference leader to make efficient use of conference time, to make progress in the discussion, preventing or avoiding mere argument that is irrelevant or talk that is repeating itself needlessly. In being properly aggressive, the leader needs good judgment and considerable sensitivity to the attitudes of the conferees. Lack of this judgment and sensitivity could cause the conferees to feel that the leader was dictatorial and arbitrary and was unwilling to have a full discussion. On the other hand, timidity on the part of the leader and delay in efforts to prevent unhelpful discussion can contribute to the waste of valuable conference time.

Conclusion. In a problem-solving conference, there should have been developed one or more proposed solutions or parts to a solution. The leader in his summary should state these clearly and obtain group (or a majority of the group) approval *again*. Then, with the help of the group, he should identify the persons or departments who have the authority to act on each separate proposal or step of a proposal. If one or more of the conferees have such authority, the leader asks such persons if they will initiate appropriate action, and when. With respect to proposed action to be taken by persons outside the conference group, the leader and the group agree on means of placing the proposals, together with any supporting data, before such persons. The members of the group are asked by the leader to commit themselves to cooperation with persons who have the authority to initiate action on the problem. In some cases the leader arranges for a report to the conference group regarding the acceptance and/or progress of their recommendations for the solving of the problem they have discussed.

The conference leader should always bear in mind that conference time invested in discussion of problems is lost time if there is no action taken on the recommended solutions to the problems.

CONSTRUCTIVE SUGGESTIONS FOR STUDENT CONFERENCE LEADERS

The student conference leaders often find it helpful to refer to a list of especially important "musts" as they progress in their training. The following is a list that has been time proved.

1. Make a challenging introduction—build a fire. Incite greater desire for action.

   a. The topic must be important; give the reason for its discussion. Usually there is an objective to be reached. Say these things briefly, concisely.

   b. Don't read the introduction; don't stammer or stutter. Don't try to memorize a given speech.

2. Prepare for the conference. It requires long experience and an agile quick-thinking mind to lead a conference with no preparation. Therefore the following procedure is recommended:

   a. Build the framework separating main from subtopics.

   b. Formulate in advance the necessary questions.

   c. Have in reserve some answers to probable questions from the group.

3. Learn how to phrase answer-provoking questions (not yes-or-no type).

4. Learn how to handle the response.

a. Understand what the conferee says, or is trying to say. Think, pay attention.
b. Don't miss or overlook something important. Someone may feel slighted.
c. If the wording is not good, help to reword it. Be a good "headline artist."
d. If the response is to be recorded, do it quickly. Cut down time spent with your back to the group.

5. Keep on top of the conference. You are the leader. Don't be sidetracked. Think ahead. Realize if an answer or discussion is in the direction you want. If not, tactfully but firmly turn it in the right direction.

6. Don't be too impatient for answers. It may be a new line of thought for the members. Take a moment more; then ask again. Don't criticize a conferee's answer or his slowness in answering. He may not try again.

7. Do not fail to summarize.

a. Don't assume a general agreement.
b. Reach some sort of conclusion.
c. State the conclusion briefly and concisely.

8. Look into the eyes of your group as you talk.
9. Pass out outline beforehand.

QUESTIONS ASKED THE CONFERENCE-LEADER TRAINER

In addition to the clinic that follows a practice conference, there may be a session devoted to answering questions that have been building up in the minds of the student leaders. The following is a list of questions asked by a student group, and the comments given by their trainer.

Question 1: Should other persons than the assigned conference group and the conference leader be present at a scheduled conference?

Comment: Other persons besides the conference leader and the discussion group may be present if there are not too many. However, the status of each visitor should be known, *i.e.*, the organization he represents and his purpose in being present, and this purpose should be such that it does not repress free discussion.

Question 2: If the one who attends the meeting as an observer or visitor takes notes or seems to, does this tend to make conferees suspect that their individual statements are being recorded and therefore cause them to limit their response?

Comment: Taking notes will often arouse curiosity. The purpose of the notes should be explained to the group. This purpose is probably a worthy one, but needs to be known in order to prevent fear of quotations and possible reprisal.

Question 3: In your opinion what effect does the presence of visitors (those who do not take part) have on the conference? Do you think that the presence of visitors might have a dampening effect on the discussion?

Comment: This question has been sufficiently answered in connection with similar questions.

Question 4: Should visitors be permitted in the conference room during the conference? If answer is affirmative, what code of ethics should be observed by such visitors?

Comment: This question, too, has been at least partially answered. It can be said further that the visitor should not attract attention. Unless he is there to participate in the discussion, he should not insert himself into the discussion at any point. He should not take notes unless the purpose of the note taking is known, understood, and approved by the conferees.

Question 5: In writing up the report of the conference, to what extent is it permissible for the conference leader to impose his own ideas or conclusions upon the listed responses?

Comment: The leader should never impose his ideas or conclusions on the conference, but, since he does have the right as one person to offer his opinion, his ideas may be added to theirs. The leader should not take advantage of his position to color or attempt to color group opinion with his own.

Question 6: If a conferee insists on a certain point to which the leader objects, what is the best procedure?

Comment: In this case the leader should record it as one person's opinion without, however, naming the person. He should not ridicule it. He should let it stand on its own merit or lack of it. If not sound, the other opinions recorded will probably show it up as being unsound.

Question 7: What is the best approach to quiet down the overtalkative conferee?

Comment: There are several possible methods. One is to always ask one or more others if they agree with a talkative person. There may be disagreements so often that he will become cautious. Another—my favorite method—is to have a private talk complimenting him by asking him for his cooperation in getting others to talk. He can be sold the idea that they need development and may also have some useful ideas.

Question 8: An entire conference group seems particularly unresponsive, answering direct questions only in one- or two-word answers. Assuming the leader has done a good job of "building the fire," what technique can be used to get the conferees to "open up"?

Comment: The leader must attempt to diagnose the reason for the group's failure to discuss freely. The reason could be, first, that it is a new problem requiring new thinking, which they cannot do too quickly. Second, the conferees may be new to a conference situation and feel some timidity or reluctance in speaking before a group. Third, there may be fear of saying something that would or could be used against them. Reasons 1 and 2 are not so serious as reason 3. Reason 1 requires questions whose answers are more obvious in order to start the thinking going. Reason 2 requires encouragement during the conference and perhaps privately between conferences. Reason 3 requires complete assurance of immunity from reprisal for frank, candid statements.

Question 9: Which is better: (*a*) to record 6 or 8 items under a given objective and promote cross-table discussion, or (*b*) to aim at recording 10 to 12 items.

Comment: The leader should make sure that each item is understood and accepted by the majority of his conferees. In fact it should be understood by all of them. So long as items come easily and rapidly, one can properly admit a long list. Only for a reason convincing to the group should the leader limit the items. There are, however, such good reasons. Some items will require cross-table discussion and may consume time. The leader's skill in getting understanding within a minimum of time will make way for other items and for the other objectives of the conference.

Question 10: How far can a conference leader go, while trying to draw out certain definite conclusions or answers, without the risk of being accused of regimentation?

Comment: The leader should not try to force his opinions even to a slight degree on his conferees. If his point of view is sound and if he is skillful, he can, by well-chosen questions rather than by mere statements, obtain acceptance even from a group at first not in agreement with him. This turns out to be a controlled or guided conference, and the leader is partly a teacher.

Question 11: Which of the following is in the best position to judge whether a conference is either good or bad, the conferees, the conference leader, or the inactive observer?

Comment: He who knows what a "good" conference is makes a better judge of a given conference. Any participant can say at once whether he liked a certain conference. He can like a very poor conference, since enthusiastic and interesting discussion is not the sole measure of goodness or badness. A conference is "good" or "bad," generally speaking, depending on whether the conference was well planned and whether worth-while conclusions were arrived at. If the leader is experienced, he is probably a better judge than the conferees, who may be basing their opinion on interesting discussion rather than upon valuable conclusions.

Question 12: If a qualified conference leader is available to attend all conferences, would not the entire program be improved by having one person conduct all the conferences? Possible improvements might be listed as follows:

Uniformity of introduction	Conclusions arrived at
Freedom of discussion	Less criticism
Use of same techniques	Economy in time of leaders

Comment: There are good reasons for sharing the load of conference leading. One reason is that it requires less time of men useful in other capacities. A second reason is that it permits use of leaders in their special fields. If all the leaders are well trained and well prepared for each conference, there should be in each case a consistent use of sound techniques, freedom of discussion, economy of time, and sound conclusions.

Question 13: With a number of conferences (20) on the same subject in each series, is it good practice to try to have them alike in outline and preliminary statement? Would not such practice tend to detract from the leader's individuality and result in responses that are essentially the same for each group?

Comment: The wording of the problem, the wording and the order of objectives, and the preliminary definitions can be the same for the different leaders, but the opening statement can and should be individual. Also, the questions and illustrations used in following the objectives throughout the discussion can be individual. These points offer sufficient opportunity for a leader's individuality. Having several people work on the preparation of a problem for discussion is a good idea. It is valuable whether there are several leaders who actually lead the conferences or only one.

Question 14: Is it not reasonable to expect that 20 conferences using the same topic and objectives will vary considerably in conclusions, owing to individual approach of the leaders, viewpoints of conferees, and other factors that cannot be entirely controlled? Is it not advisable, therefore, to have each individual conference stand on its own feet? Should not the final minutes, instead of being a summary of the 20 conferences, copy conclusions reached by each conference, indicating them by group number, thereby permitting conferees to compare their own decisions with those of the other groups?

Comment: It is suggested that to save repetition, it is better to make a composite report including every different item. This can be done for each list developed in the conference and for the final conclusions. It is also a justifiable effort and expense to furnish each group a separate listing of their own items. In some cases the individual items in the composite report are coded to show from which group they came. Any one item may be coded with several code marks to show that it came from more than one group. This has the advantage of showing a group their own lists as compared with the larger composite units.

Question 15: If the leader realizes that some foremen have "gripes" of their own that they believe to be general, but realizes, too, that the immediate problems of the foremen cannot be developed to a satisfactory conclusion because of the limited time allotted for the conference and because of the nature of the group in attendance, which is the better policy for the leader to follow out:

a. Stick to simple and generalized conclusions?

b. Develop one specific conclusion as much as time will permit, and refer the subject to higher management or a special committee for further study and solution?

Comment: "Gripes" as such, if recognized, should be discouraged by the leader. A gripe may be well founded and shared by others, but do not permit this gripe to extend into a prolonged discussion. Use it as proof of or the substance of a recorded item and move on to the next item. In answer to question (*a*), one cannot and should not try to play safe by generalizing too much. People usually like to get down to cases, since doing so makes the discussion more interesting. In answer to question (*b*), if the reasoning and the specific conclusion are sound, it is a definite accomplishment, and better than several generalizations. Alternative conclusions may be proposed, depending upon points of view represented in the conference group. Time limitations may prevent full discussion, however.

Question 16: To date, our objectives have been kept quite simple and somewhat obvious. Is it practical and safe to narrow subjects or objectives down to immediate problems? Examples are

Inequities in pay, particularly supervisor vs. worker.

Specific authority of the foreman in handling grievances at source.

Centralized maintenance as compared with departmental maintenance.

(It is feared that a number of foremen will not long be satisfied with platitudes or be willing to take the time to discuss them, unless they can see probable specific and direct benefits to their own pay or working conditions.)

Comment: Sometimes some problems may have to wait for an opportune time for frank discussion, but eventually every problem, no matter how controversial, should be faced frankly and courageously. The stage may have to be prepared by investigations or by additions to, or revisions of, policy, but the real problem must be faced and not delayed too long. This is really very important.

Question 17: Is it safe for the conference leader to attempt to steer the trend of discussion when it is obvious that two or more conferees have a "bone to pick" and will not be satisfied if they are not permitted to proceed to the point where some suggestions are recorded or action decided upon?

Comment: If the bone to be picked is irrelevant to the conference objectives, the leader has the right to tactfully but firmly rule it out. He must be sure, however, that it is irrelevant before ruling it out. Perhaps the "bone" is one of the parts or angles of the problem, in which case suitable discussion and records are justified. A good rule to follow is to be too lenient instead of too strict, but no rule is a substitute for good judgment on the leader's part.

Question 18: In starting a conference, should the conference leader spend a few moments putting the conferees at ease or start the conference immediately by giving the problem and making the introductory statement?

Comment: If the leader and the conferees are new to one another, time taken in becoming acquainted and getting comfortably at ease is time well spent. No good work will be done by a group or by an individual member who is not at ease. If the group and the leader have worked together through several conferences, the leader can start the conference with 30 seconds to a minute or so of "settling down" comment.

Question 19: During a conference a relevant cross-table discussion participated in by two or more conferees may develop. Is it good leadership to allow this conversation to run itself out, or should the conference leader tactfully attempt to break up the conversation?

Comment: The conference leader should not attempt to break it up; rather, he should seek to have it become more general, especially if he sees evidence of someone's trying or wanting to join the cross-table discussion. The leader must be alert to recognize when it has gone far enough, and then he should move smoothly to the next item or objective. He may often interrupt a cross-table discussion to have a point clarified so that all of the group can understand what is being said or implied.

Question 20: Under our conference plan, in which a series of conferences are given on the same problem, would it not be an advantage to let the responses develop as they will so that the general thought of the group will become apparent? There seems to be a tendency to lead the conferees into a more or less prescribed channel. Does this not defeat to some extent the true value of the conference program?

Comment: There should be no curb on an individual's thought processes. If his contribution is relevant to the objective being developed, however different or original his idea may be, it can be used. If it is a border-line case, and the leader is not sure whether it is a valuable contribution, it can be so identified. If actually irrelevant, it can usually be convincingly shown to be such, and in that event is not recorded.

Question 21: When a lull occurs in which none of the conferees seem inclined to talk, is it good practice to wait them out? After a little time someone will talk, and usually the conference goes on pretty well from there.

Comment: An experienced conference leader will nearly always know whether the silence is caused by thinking that is preparatory to speech or caused by the fact that the conferees' minds are at a standstill. In the latter case he must start them thinking again by means of another question, an illustration, or a quick summary of what has just been said followed by a question whose answer is not too difficult. Forward motion and conference progress will then be resumed.

Question 22: Which is better procedure:

You have made a list of faults covered by an objective. Now it is time to discuss and list solutions or improvements for future practice.

Should the leader take time to further discuss and record the reverse of each fault listed?

Should he encourage a statement of reversing faults to positive action and continue to secure more items general to the solution to the problem?

Comment: In many, probably in most, cases the reverse of a list of faults is so obvious that the listing becomes anti-climatic, too easy to be interesting; only in those items where the "how" or the details of the remedy are in doubt is a discussion well worth while. The obvious ones can be briefly noted.

Because this reverse-list procedure ignores new and original helpful suggestions, the leader should call for and stimulate the original thinking that brings out such new and helpful suggestions, even after he has listed the reverse items.

Part 2

HOW TO USE A CONFERENCE PROGRAM

Before discussing the use of a conference program, it is necessary to discuss first the entire training program, of which the conference program is a part. There are a great many things to be said as a basis or foundation for the presentation of How to Use a Conference Program. It cannot be safely assumed that these things will be remembered or even realized without recording them here. Therefore the next four chapters are used to prepare for detailed discussion regarding the use of conferences and a conference program.

CHAPTER 11

NEED FOR A PLANNED AND COMPLETE TRAINING PROGRAM

TRAINING NEEDS CAUSED BY INCREASING COMPLEXITY

Occupational training for the entire organization is regarded by the wise modern factory executive as a necessary program that pays dividends just as truly as expenditures for tools, supplies, power, heating, lighting and ventilating, wages for employees, or any other expense that is taken for granted. In the era in which we live, scientific research and common everyday trial and error have developed procedures and processes that require skill and job know-how far above the level of unskilled labor. And the end of this industrial development, which has resulted in a higher standard of living for our nation as a whole, is not even in sight. Our industries will continue to invent and to improve methods and procedures and will develop the tools and machines to match them. The skill of workers will increase and also change in character, adapting itself to the newest procedures and processes. The methods and machines of yesterday are obsolete tomorrow for they constantly are being replaced by new methods and new machines. The new methods and machines may or may not be more complicated than the old, but in either case that which is new must be learned. The level of skill and know-how will not decline.

For many decades industries grew and thrived without very much organized training. They did not see the need for it. For one thing, competition was not so keen: there were more frontiers where pioneering could succeed, regardless of how inefficient it was. Organizations were smaller, skill and information were passed on by those at the head of the organization much more readily than today, and having experienced workers teach new workers the relatively few things the new worker needed to know in order to "get by" worked out with enough success that industry generally grew rapidly.

The industrial organizations of yesterday can be compared to the high-school and small-college football teams of 40 years ago. There were few professional full-time coaches. The rules were few and primitive. The teams were not well drilled and trained and were not made execution-perfect, as is the intention today. There was not a very high degree of intelligence required to play football. If a boy were big and strong he was sought as a player, and if he were among the biggest and strongest, he was probably a star, for he could plow through the opposing team's line by sheer power.

Today the game of football is very, very different. It has become a complicated game made up of a great number of intricate plays. Full-time professional coaches with a full-time staff (in universities at least) spend hours every day training the players. Strength and size are assets in football of today, but even more important is the intelligence of the player. Many players of medium stature are stars.

The best football teams of even 15 years ago (to say nothing of teams of 25 years ago) probably could not score on third-rate teams today, and would be overwhelmed by tremendous scores. The reason would be training and job know-how.

COMPETITION REQUIRES TRAINING AND CO-OPERATION

Modern industry is very much like modern football. Competition is intense. Advantages of monopoly are few and becoming fewer. Because many organizations produce similar products, these organizations contest with each other to do the best job and produce the best buy for the customers. The aim of each organization is to give the most or at least the same quality for the least cost. For this reason, workers need to be trained to save seconds as well as minutes, to develop the skill that makes quality even slightly better, to reduce scrap and rework, to care for delicate, complicated, and costly machines, and to conserve power. Always they must be trained for personal safety. Workers need to be trained in their mental attitudes. They need to understand the principles of industrial organization, such as mutual dependence of owner and employee, their common interests, what teamwork really consists of. On a successful football team there are often players who do not personally like some of the other players; this personal liking may be lacking between the coach and some of the players. But, in a game, each does his assigned part, and when the team wins each has the personal reward and satisfaction of victory. So in industry, in a given organization it is not "in the cards" for every employee among hundreds or thousands to like everyone else and for every foreman, superintendent, and factory manager to be personally liked by all who work for and with him. But training can make the foreman, superintendent, or factory manager liked by *more* of his coworkers than if he has no such training. Training can prevail upon workers at any level to be more understanding, and therefore more tolerant, more cooperative, and more efficient and valuable team members (employees).

TRAINING AS AN INVESTMENT

Regardless of their attitudes toward training in general for the worker, industrial organizations for years have recognized the importance of training for safety. Large sums have and are being spent for safety. Money spent for safety is not dependent on a minimum financial return for the dollars invested. Who can tell how many lives are saved, how many limbs are saved, how many man-hours of employment are saved, how much physical suffering is saved, how much privation and want for injured workers' families is saved by safety training? The money expended for safety programs is universally assumed to be well spent, without accounting in terms of dollar profit.

However, training for job skills and attitudes needs wider acceptance than it has today. It needs to be recognized that every worker, from production worker, sweeper, and maintenance worker to factory manager, can do better than he is doing, and that improvement of even a small degree can often mean the difference between winning from or losing to competition. Winning or losing is often by small margins. A small saving in time, or in some other item of cost, multiplied by the pieces produced and sold, often runs into very large sums of money, and this saving is shared by all who contribute their physical and mental effort.

It needs to be recognized that with the very small per cent of income per invested dollar, industry exists precariously. Up to the present many organizations have remained in business with little or no organized training. But who knows what would have been the limit of earnings if training had been used? Not one of the many thousands of industrial organizations who have had no formal training programs can answer that question.

They have yet to learn what a comparatively few industrial executives have already learned: Training does not *cost* money, training helps to *make* money. Only *lack of training* costs real money. Those organizations which have an intelligently planned training program believe in it and will not part with it. More executives are seeing the light; still more need to see it.

TRAINING FOR PROBLEMS OF SCHOOL ORGANIZATIONS

In school organizations it is becoming more and more evident that the personnel at all levels need on-the-job training. Teachers and administrators have received professional training in how to teach, how to build courses of study and curricula, how to administer. But this necessary professional training does not deal with relationships between teachers, between teachers and parents, between teachers and principals and superintendents. It does not deal with extracurricular activities, such as sponsoring and chaperoning student social functions. The professional training does not answer such important questions as, How can principals and superintendents be of more practical help to the teachers in their local situation? How can friction between parents and the school organization be avoided? Should a merit-rating or similar plan be made a part of the salary plan for this school-city organization? These problems need to be solved in order to maintain progress. Many problems are solved by discussion, and participation in problem-solving discussions (conferences) is a form of individual training. Participation in conferences trains an individual in thinking and reasoning, and contributes a great amount of useful information that can be profitably used many times.

Another group of persons in the school organization is that group that cares for buildings and grounds. It has been popularly believed that a janitor (custodian) does not need to know anything and that anyone can be a janitor. This is not true. There are inefficient and efficient methods for care and maintenance. The physical-plant employees can be classed today as skilled specialists, if they are given planned adequate training. There are materials and tools designed for cleaning and maintenance, and their proper use deserves and demands adequate training. Also, there are rules and policies to understand and to follow, and these are more certainly accepted and followed if they are presented through an organized plan and the reasons back of them are frankly explained. Such training in skills and attitudes would save in operational and maintenance costs of the physical plant.

In conclusion, an on-the-job training program for school organizations would be to the self-interest of every group in the community. Teachers and administrators and physical-plant employees would be more efficient, and would enjoy their work more than without such a program. The students would directly benefit as a result of better teacher influence in mutual relationships outside the classroom. The school board and citizens would benefit by better and more complete training of future citizens and public officials.

CHAPTER 12

EVALUATION OF TRAINING PROGRAMS

The introduction of training programs to modern industry has been retarded to some extent by the lack of measurement of the results obtained. There has been very little authentic evaluation of training programs. If there were more scientifically conducted evalutions of training programs, more managements would adopt training as a permanent program.

There are at least two methods of evaluating training. One of these is by means of a before-and-after measurement, the other is by means of a control group. A description of how each of these methods of measurement could be carried out should help one to understand the two methods.

In the before-and-after method of measurement, the efficiency of a selected group is measured over two equal periods of time, first without benefit of training, and next after training has been given. Care must be taken to ensure as far as is possible exactly identical conditions of work, the only differences being the lack of training in the first period and the benefit of training in the second period. The length of the trial periods should be long enough to ensure that all normal work conditions are experienced, and short enough to eliminate as far as possible the danger of factors or conditions coming into one trial period and not in the other. The longer the period, the greater will be the danger of dissimilarity of work conditions and other factors. Informed opinion of persons experienced in tests covering various periods of time seems to favor periods of 30 to 60 working days for a measurement of the type discussed here. It should be understood that in the before-and-after method of measurement of the value of training, in which one group is used, the training period itself is an interlude between the two test periods. It would not be fair or conclusive to use the training period itself as the second or "after" period. The reasons for this should be obvious.

In the method using a control group, two or more groups may be measured simultaneously. The control group has no benefit of training; the other or others have had the benefit of training. The groups that have the advantage of training may have different amounts or types of training. Measurement of these groups that vary in training would be useful in evaluating how much training to give a group, or which of two types of training is preferable. In conducting a test for this purpose, all possible care should be taken to have identical conditions and factors existing in all groups, except for the differences in training. The use of different groups introduces differences in human traits and abilities, and these can never be entirely equalized. This does not mean that this method is undesirable or impracticable, but it does mean that it must be used with great care and preferably by experienced persons.

It should be worth the while of many organizations, particularly those that have large numbers of employees, to prove to themselves the value of training, if they are unwilling to accept the opinions and evidence now available from organizations who do maintain permanent training programs. Either or both of the methods briefly presented here may be more fully investigated and used to suit the needs of the individual organization.

CHAPTER 13

A PHILOSOPHY FOR INDUSTRIAL AND SCHOOL ORGANIZATION TRAINING

VARIOUS CONCEPTS OF TRAINING

Too often industrial organizations maintain a form of training that is inadequate or poorly planned. Concepts regarding what training is vary greatly from person to person and from organization to organization. In some organizations only training at the worker level is emphasized, and this training is concerned mostly with the various job skills and related information needed for the production jobs. This may be the fault of the training director, or it may be the fault of the management, which may limit the activities and projects of the training director. Such training does not recognize the necessity for attitude training of production workers. Workers who do not understand modern industrial economics cannot realize the effect of wasting time, being needlessly absent, abusing equipment, etc., and need attitude correction through appropriate education. Correct attitudes are even more valuable than job skills. Not only is the worker training that does not include attitude training inadequate, but limiting training to workers shows a lack of recognition of the needs of other groups in the organization.

Industrial or plant training is thought of by some management and training personnel as management training that emphasizes foremen training. It may include training in the various duties of foremen, such as how to get out production, how to reduce scrap and waste, how to maintain equipment, how to delegate responsibility, how to correct workers, and how to handle grievances. Even though this foremen training is well organized and presented, if it goes no further it is too narrow. There is always the need for attitude development. Furthermore, other levels of management also need training appropriate to their level and to the type of duties performed.

In some organizations safety and housekeeping may receive the most attention by those responsible for training. And this training may be confined to the production-worker level. If so, it is too narrow even for safety and housekeeping. Office workers and all levels of management need this training, which should include attitude training. There are hazards in offices, and office workers need training in how to deal with such hazards. Top management must be known to be behind safety training, and they must set the example in practicing safety.

WHEN AND HOW LONG TO PROVIDE TRAINING

Not only may training be inadequate in that it fails to include all groups in the organization and to include attitude forming, but it may be lacking in that it fails to recognize an important principle, that of *when* to give training. Too often so-called "training" is the "lock the barn after the horse is stolen" type. Training is not thought of until things go wrong. In other words, it is regarded solely as remedial. This is an incorrect concept. Such training will never be adequate or fully satisfactory. A sounder concept is that training is preventive. It prevents (if it is well done) an endless series of losses of the same kind due to the same causes. Preventive training is the kind that begins with the new worker on a new assignment and continues until that worker has attained standards of performance well above the minimum. This training covers all phases of job techniques and related information, and does not overlook attitude training.

After adequate training has been given to new employees and to old employees with new jobs, there should be a follow-up program. It cannot be safely assumed that all persons adequately trained will continue indefinitely to perform their tasks in keeping with this training. Some individuals will be tempted to short-cut a procedure in order to save time or effort, or to turn out more finished work. Some will try out ideas of their own without telling them to their foreman or trainer. In other cases there will be changes made in tools, machines, procedures, materials, or any combination of these. The workers cannot be expected to take these changes in stride. They will need help in the form of additional training which will teach them to handle proficiently the new tools or procedures.

The conduct of a training program is an investment that eliminates long periods of slow improvement in efficiency and lessens the danger of many workers making little or no progress in efficiency after they have reached minimum job standards. It reduces greatly the amount of product spoiled and lost due to poor workmanship and the amount of rework performed to reclaim the product. Not only is this policy of preventive training good for workers, but it is even better for management. The results of no training or of inadequate training are far more costly in the case of a foreman or a factory manager than in the case of a worker at the production level. The errors of the foreman or factory manager will in most cases affect the performance of all persons responsible to him.

SPECIAL TRAINING METHODS OF SCHOOL PERSONNEL

The preceding paragraphs have dealt with training in industrial organizations. The same principles apply to school organizations. There are many duties of teachers for which the teacher has often had no training. The teachers often have no training in extracurricular activities, such as sponsoring and chaperoning student social activities or working in parent-teacher associations. They often have no training for duties and assignments in public relations (where the teacher is representing the school system to the public), such as appearing in forums or taking part in other civic activities. Training is needed to improve the relationships between teachers themselves, between teachers and principals, between the teachers and principals and the superintendents, and between teachers and pupils outside the classroom. Training is needed by persons employed to care for buildings and grounds, by secretaries and office workers generally. Most school organizations are large and need their own training programs to give on-the-job training apart from the professional training of the teacher. Each school building is a unit, and in it work a principal, teachers, one or more secretaries, librarians, and building custodians. Within the school city there are often many such units.

In the school city the total number of employed persons (superintendents, principals, teachers, secretaries, librarians, custodial personnel) often runs into the hundreds and sometimes thousands. The amount of training needed by these many persons, apart from the professional teacher training, is tremendous. The author takes this occasion to recommend to the medium-sized and larger school cities that they consider adding a training program with a full-time director of training to guide and direct the program. It would pay dividends in the form of more complete training of teachers, particularly in various attitudes; and in the case of custodial personnel it would save in physical-plant operation and maintenance. The taxpayers could very probably have a better operated school system with no more funds than at present.

In conclusion, it is recommended that in a school or industrial organization the proper concept for training of personnel, the on-the-job training apart from professional training, should conform to three principles as follows:

1. The training should include all persons in the organization, from the highest-ranking executive to the lowest-paid worker.

2. The training should be primarily preventive training with follow-up.

3. Attitude training at all levels should be given as needed.

With a training program so conceived and conscientiously administered, there would be better human relations, more personal and organization efficiency, and more real job happiness for individuals.

CHAPTER 14

THE PLACE OF A CONFERENCE PROGRAM IN THE TOTAL TRAINING PROGRAM

It has been stated that an adequate program of on-the-job training for either school organizations or industrial organizations should include every person in the organization from the chief executive to the lowest-paid worker. The training, to be adequate, will not omit any need of the individual, whether it be for job skill, for related information, or for attitude improvement and development. With respect to the place of a conference program in the total program, two major factors need consideration.

The first factor to be considered is the content or subject matter of the training. Some training is needed for technical information, for formulas, or for step-by-step procedures in an operation. Examples are the training of a research assistant in the chemistry of rubber or in metallurgy, the training of an assistant bookkeeper, and the training of an operator of a machine. The information and skill involved are not yet in the possession of the new employee. He cannot respond and contribute, as do participants in a conference. He needs the aid of an instructor who can explain and demonstrate and then supervise his (the new employee's) first efforts. The instructor-learner relationship may be limited to the instructor and one learner, or several learners may be instructed at the same time.

Some training is for the purpose of understanding policies, for solving problems that are common to a number of people, or for building or correcting attitudes. For example, there may be the need to understand a new or revised policy. The conference procedure applies here. A conference group of foremen listen to the statement of a new or revised policy and are then asked to state how this will affect them in their individual departments. Their individual replies call forth approval or disagreement on the part of the other conference participants, including the leader. Under the direction of the leader, the discussion continues until the right interpretation is understood by everyone and consistent application is provided for. Another example is the need to solve a production problem, which could be that of improving the efficiency of the unloading and warehousing of raw materials. Persons sharing in this problem participate in a conference, each participant contributing his experience and thinking. The discussion continues under the guidance of the conference leader until specific recommendations are reached and agreed upon. The conference is the logical training medium here.

The second factor that must be considered with respect to the place of a conference program in the total program is the rank of the individuals who require training. In most cases the conference plan is a better medium of training for all levels of management. Management is more skilled in thinking and in discussion than are the men and women in production or in routine office tasks. The conference plan uses thinking and discussion ability, and, to any person, participating in a conference is more appealing than attending a class, in which the students receive, and do not contribute to, the course content.

The training of persons in production jobs or routine tasks is usually that of training in job skills and related information, and this requires the instructor-learner relationship previously referred to. However, there is an increasing need to improve and develop attitudes of workers, and this is best done through discussion. Worker conferences intended to present, and to aid in the understanding of, modern industrial economics (for one example) are recommended.

The immediately preceding paragraphs refer to industrial training programs. In school-city organizations the training of the administrative and teaching staff should be, for the most part, of the conference type because the content of the training is that of policy and rules interpretation, of problem solving, and of attitude development. Also, the administrators and teachers are persons trained in thinking and in oral presentation of ideas. These two factors indicate the choice of conferences for the training medium.

With respect to building custodians and others employed to maintain the physical plant, the instructor-learner relationship is recommended for the training of job skills and related information. For the training of attitude improvement and development, the conference method is recommended.

From the foregoing paragraphs it should be evident that the conference plan of training plays a very large and significant part in training programs for industry and for the employees of a school city. The conference is especially appropriate for problem solving and for training in thinking and attitude building, regardless of the rank of the persons involved. Because industrial management personnel and the teachers and administrators of school organizations face problems to be solved, policies to be decided upon and interpreted, and attitudes to be formed, it is for them the most useful training medium. It is not desirable or necessary to compare the worth of the conference method and the instructor-learner method of training. Both are necessary and neither one can satisfactorily substitute for the other. In some organizations and at certain periods their use may be nearly equal so far as the number of persons trained by the two methods is concerned. In other situations either one may be used more extensively than the other. Both should be used to the extent necessary to ensure adequate training of all persons in all levels of the organization.

CHAPTER 15

EFFECTIVE USE OF A CONFERENCE PROGRAM

PRIMARY USES OF CONFERENCE PROGRAMS

Industrial executives and school administrators who have given conference programs a reasonable trial regard them as valuable tools. Many who have not given them a trial have a good opinion of them. This latter group probably outnumbers the group who through experience know the value of conference programs, but because of inertia, procrastination, or ignorance of how to build for such a program, have no program of their own. There are probably other factors that explain the failure of various groups to have conference programs.

Conference programs accomplish two kinds of objectives. They help to solve problems; and they are a means of helping individual participants to develop and to improve themselves, for a conference program can be used to train and educate persons, to improve their performance and their attitudes. Attitudes greatly affect job performance. Any tools that help to solve an organization's problems, that improve skill and attitudes and on-the-job performance, are worth having, even though the tools cost real money.

THE PROBLEM-SOLVING CONFERENCE

Let us consider the first kind of objective of the conference program, problem solving. Problems affect one or more persons, usually more than one. Frequently 5 or 10 or 20 persons are directly affected by a common problem, and the entire organization is indirectly affected. Rather than attempt singly to solve the problem, it is common sense to "gang up" on it. Single-handed attacks too often collide with one another or are ineffective because a good idea is not taken to the others concerned, is therefore not supported, and eventually dies. Suppose, however, all the persons concerned have a meeting. Called in all seriousness and with the best of intentions, the meeting can, and too often does, result in arguments, accusations, rebuttals, alibis, increased mental temperatures, and strained relations. The most frequent causes for this unhappy ending to a meeting called to consider a problem are, first, the lack of a trained conference leader who knows how to prepare for a problem-solving conference, and, second, the ignorance of the persons involved in the problem regarding how individually to participate in a problem-solving conference. Individually, the persons involved in the problem are probably sincere, have initiative, and have some good ideas; but each one lacks some experience and information possessed by some others in the group, and does not know how to obtain it in problem-solving conferences.

There may be another reason for the failure of a meeting. A high-ranking executive may call a meeting (not a conference) of his subordinates, proceed to say, "I think . . . ," outline his personal solution, give instructions regarding how to put his plan into effect, and adjourn the meeting without asking his subordinates for their constructive suggestions. His plan may be excellent. But it is good insurance to subject it to analysis by other experienced persons. It may have a weakness that can be discovered and mended.

Through skilled conference leadership, a confident and skilled team works together to attack a problem, with each team member making his own significant contribution of experience and thinking and willingly accepting the helpful experience and thinking of his teammates. There is give and take and compromise in a democratic discussion. Out of it comes a solution for the problem, probably not perfect or entirely acceptable to every person, but accepted by the majority as being workable and an improvement over the present conditions. This result is possible because the trained conference leader knows how to draw from each conference participant that which he can contribute to the pool of information and experience regarding the problem. And then, when the miscellaneous contributions have been made, the trained leader aids and directs the group in sorting and appraising the contributions and in fitting them into a workable solution. The leader himself could not solve the problem unaided, but with his special ability to organize and direct the attack, the entire team is successful. The preceding statement is true whether the problem is one of production or in the field of human relations.

THE ATTITUDE-BUILDING CONFERENCE

Let us now consider the attitude-building conference, or the educational type of conference. In this type of conference real problems are discussed, but the solution calls for thinking that is new to the participants. This is difficult for individuals who have been engaged in routine tasks, with no responsibilities for creative effort. The conference leader in this situation is more of a teacher than in a problem-solving conference, yet he does not lecture. Instead, he asks a series of carefully prepared questions, beginning with the primary steps of reasoning, repeating the question or changing the form of the question until the needed and previously planned statement is offered by someone in the group. In this way the carefully drawn-out facts (not opinions) are presented in proper sequence and are formed into a reasonably clear composite picture in the mind of each conference member. Now understanding has been brought about, attitudes have been molded without the individual conference members being conscious of the fact.

As an illustration, a group of foremen in an organization making a first start in conducting a conference program were led to discuss the economic costs of workers' failure to do a full day's work, workers' excessive absenteeism, and workers' resistance to job-methods improvement. The foremen were at once greatly interested and with the conference leader developed lists of economic costs. They were then asked who paid these costs. They quickly came to the realization that the customer paid them. When asked who the customers were, they came to the realization that they (the foremen) and the workers were part of the great body of buyers of a product whose price could have been less had workers done a full day's work, avoided unnecessary absence, and not opposed better job methods. These foremen made all the positive statements in that conference. The leader actually made none, only asked questions. Each foreman had at various times recognized these facts singly but had never had a picture of all of these facts related to each other as they were in the conference under the guidance of a trained leader. These foremen had a taste of industrial economics. They talked about it with their workers, as well as with one another. Some of them talked about it at home, and the children told their schoolteachers about it. The foremen wanted more of the same kind of conferences. The senior management was glad to oblige.

LEADERSHIP FOR THE PROGRAM

Some organizations have training supervisors or directors in charge of the organization's training program. Others use a steering committee. Still others have little formal planning and conferences are irregular, not coordinated, and the effort is hardly worthy of the name of a program. If the policy-making executive or executives wish to have a conference program that more than pays for itself, it is only common sense to make the program a major responsibility of some person or some group. The author prefers this responsibility to be given to one person. This person, whose title may be supervisor of training or training director (or some other suitable title), should report to the plant manager or to the production manager.*

Because the responsibility for a successful conference program is one that requires considerable time and effort, this assignment should never be made an extra on top of an already full load. There should be a rearrangement of assignments so that the responsibility for the conference program can be discharged on company time without any other responsibility being slighted. Attempting to squeeze in the responsibility for a conference program with a full load of other duties is shortsighted: it is unfair to the person given the assignment and unfair to the program. An overloaded person will sooner or later slight some of his assignments, and the major share of the blame belongs to his superior officer.

The training director should approach his problem carefully and make thorough preparation. As in a city vocational-education program where a survey of community needs is made before building a program, so in industry the training director should survey the training needs of his organization. He should question top-rank executives and all subordinate levels of management. He should talk to production workers. Always he is seeking difficulties and problems that seem to keep on occurring, seeking evidence of unsatisfactory working conditions and seeking evidence of unsatisfactory policies. He wants to know the skills needed in the various levels of management and in various service departments, and he wants to know the specific shortcomings or problems of special groups.

After the survey is complete, program planning begins. A decision must be reached regarding how comprehensive the conference program will be, *i.e.*, how many people from what groups or levels will be included, how the conference groups will be made up, how often conferences will be held, and what specific conference problems will be discussed and

* See "The Place of the Training Director in Industry," *Factory Management and Maintenance,* March, 1945.

in what sequence. It will be necessary to have a trained conference leader or a number of leaders. If the organization has no trained leaders, they must be trained, or leaders already trained must be employed. It is good policy to train persons within the organization so that they will be available for a continuing program. Other decisions include the selection and preparation of the conference room and the selection of the days and hours when the conference will be held.

In beginning a program, it is better to start modestly as to size, do a good job to develop respect for the program, and expand as the need and facilities indicate. Some key persons may be doubtful regarding the worth of a program, and it may require convincing proof to get them to support, and cooperate with, the program. The length of a year's program should be carefully considered. It is not wise to conduct a full program every week in the year. There should be no program fatigue, and to avoid this the program may well be halted for 8 to 12 weeks, preferably in the summer months.

Not only is a survey needed to initiate a program, but surveys must be continued to keep the program up to date. The training director should maintain contacts with key persons and become informed regarding the kind of problems they have. He should be alert to observe conditions so that in many cases he can suggest that certain problems be included in the program.

A very able and competent training director asked for and was granted the privilege of attending staff meetings conducted by top-rank executives, including sales, inspection, returned goods, and many production meetings. In one session he learned that a certain product was causing excessive customer dissatisfaction, and the product was being returned to the factory in unprecedented volumes. He invited a group of key persons to the conference room to discuss the causes back of this condition. In this conference, which he personally conducted, it was brought out that the product was returned for not one, but for several reasons. It was brought out that the inspectors had been recruited from worker ranks and had received no planned training. As a result, among the inspectors there was no consistent inspection. The training director proposed a course of instruction (which he would have prepared) for the instructors and a check-up on how well the workers on this product were following standard procedures and methods. The suggestions were accepted, were acted upon, and at the end of approximately 60 days the problem had ceased to exist.

FOLLOW-UP

It should be recognized that conferences may propose excellent answers to problems. But the answers do not automatically work out themselves. They must be worked out by the individuals concerned. Follow-up is required to see that this is done. The training director should follow up his conferences or delegate this particular responsibility. He should see that proposals or recommendations are put in the hands of people who make decisions, if such are required. He should do all he can to get prompt decisions and prompt action. Delayed decisions and delayed action discourage the groups that make the recommendations.

At this point it is appropriate to present a report of a conference called to consider how to use the ability of a group of newly trained conference leaders.

REPORT OF WORK CONFERENCE

Jan. 16, 1946

Problem: How can we use our trained conference leaders as a management tool?

Objectives:

1. To examine some conference-leader skills offered by this trained group.

2. To examine some practical management uses of these skills and attendant benefits.

3. To recommend a tentative program to use conference leaders effectively.

Definitions: "Trained conference leaders" are persons who have actively participated in a conference-leader training program and need only additional thoughtful experience and helpful guidance.

A "management tool" is any person, program, process, or thing which can be used to achieve an objective of management.

Opening Statement: We have reached the point where we should begin to know what are the skills of the conference leaders and how these skills can be useful to management. The trained conference leaders are rapidly approaching the time when they will move from training conference to actual work conferences.

It appears then that it is time for us to begin to think about how management can use the skills implanted in or partially developed in this group because, it seems to me, this problem is becoming "hot." We are being asked to discuss it in this conference.

Management has approved this training program because they were convinced by someone that it would pay dividends and that it would develop a valuable tool for the use of management. If you have done any thinking about the question of the cost of this program and if you have arrived at some rough estimate, you will have discovered that the cost of the program must be measured in thousands rather than hundreds of dollars. Not too many thousands it is true, but enough to represent an investment that we cannot afford to throw away lightly.

The members of this training group were deliberately chosen by management to take this training because management had confidence in each individual's ability and willingness to profit by the training. It seems then that we as a group and as individuals have a responsibility to management to furnish the trainees the tools which they have wanted and which they have planned to develop through this training program.

In order to be of some assistance to the group, the leader has prepared the objectives that you will see on the panel to the right, namely: (1) to examine some conference-leader skills offered by this trained group, (2) to examine some practical management uses of these skills and attendant benefits, (3) to recommend a tentative program to use conference leaders effectively. Is there any question or comment from the group on the statement of the conference problem or on the objectives? Do you feel that these objectives will permit us to move in a profitable direction? (No questions or objections were offered by the group.)

Discussion: In order to assist us in starting from a common point of departure, two definitions are prepared in tentative form. I have chosen to tentatively define "trained conference leaders" as persons who have actively participated in a conference-leader training program and need only additional thoughtful experience and helpful guidance. It is proposed that you underline in your own thinking the words "actively participated."

The phrase "management tool" is defined as any person, program, process, or thing that can be used to achieve an objective of management. (The group was invited to comment on or amend these definitions, but no amendments were offered.)

In order to save some time and for your convenience, a tentative list of conference-leader skills has been prepared for your consideration under the first objective. Suppose we take a look at this list of skills. If any of them represent, in your opinion, wishful thinking or an unrealistic appraisal of conference-leader training, you are urged to bring that to the attention of the group.

SKILLS

1. Recognize and select topic problems.
2. Separate problem causes from symptoms.
3. Present problems in clear and challenging terms.
4. Establish common grounds for discussion.

5. Spark a group's desire to think about and discuss common problems.

6. Lead the groups from the problem to both specific and over-all planning.

7. Draw out and point up group experience and thinking.

8. Pool and summarize group experience and thinking.

9. Develop unified thought and action from hazy, diverse ideas.

10. Record contributions to aid group thinking.

11. Keep group thinking "on the beam" and save group time.

12. Lead the individual conference in such a way as to benefit the group.

13. Read the real meaning behind or beyond face value of statements.

14. Sample and interpret group and individual opinion and feeling.

15. Lead the group upon occasion to willingly approve predetermined conclusions.

16. Develop tolerance and open-mindedness in the group.

17. Summarize and bring into sharp focus group conclusions.

18. Lead the group to set up adequate machinery for getting action.

19. Improve knowledge and skill as an instructor, trainer, or teacher.

(The last item in the above list was an addition made by the group.) The entire list was discussed and it is to be emphasized that it was the unanimous feeling of this group that probably no one individual conference leader possesses any one of these skills in its entirety. Neither does he possess every one of these skills to any great extent. It was emphasized that management should, in planning the use of the conference tool, recognize the limitations, noted in our definition, of a trained conference leader and further recognize that this list of skills represents incipient or "seeling" skills, which will grow and develop in terms of individual effort and opportunity for exercise.

With these thoughts in mind the group began discussion of objective 2, consideration of possible, practical management uses of these skills and the benefits that would attend, in the group's opinion, the use of these skills.

It should be pointed out that the benefits considered by the group in the discussion of objective 2 are not the benefits that would occur from solving the problem or from achieving management's major objectives in a given situation. The benefits listed here are only those benefits that the group felt would result from using conference techniques and conference-leader skills in attacking the problem rather than using more traditional methods of attack. In short, the benefits listed are the benefits of holding conferences over and above such other benefits as would result from solving the problem involved.

Practical Uses	Attendant Benefits
Identify, clarify, and remedy or solve basic problems or causes of grievances*	1. More thorough understanding of the factors involved by a larger number of people 2. A better chance of arriving at agreement on sound basis 3. Conclusions and results are felt to be a group achievement rather than the work of a few individuals 4. The conference method permits and encourages or even demands wider participation, which affords a better chance of bringing to light and to consideration all facts and factors

* It was pointed out by the group that this involves primarily the field of human relations, and that the problems or causes of grievances referred to may be observed before the grievances arise or may be identified after a formal grievance has been lodged.

Practical Uses	Attendant Benefits
	5. Much repetition from one department to another may be avoided 6. Treatment of a problem tends to be more impersonal and unbiased 7. Defensive tactics are reduced 8. In general, there is an over-all saving of time
Amendment or development of policies or the local application of over-all policies that lie within the jurisdiction of plant management; the development of recommendations regarding policy development or suggested amendments for submission to the policy-making body	1. Each conference participant comes to feel that he has a part in policy making and application and that such policies are, in effect, his own work 2. Such policy or policy applications tend to be more workable because they stand upon a broader base of information and agreement 3. A better understanding is likely to result 4. A more ready acceptance is likely to be achieved 5. A greater feeling of participation in a democratic process results
To explain or clarify policies or policy applications	1. A more uniform application based on better understanding and wider appreciation of the many factors involved will frequently result*
As a method of training or as a training-program†	1. Better group and individual participation because the par-

* It was pointed out by the group that many of the benefits already listed will also apply in this particular use.

It was emphasized by the group that conferences for this particular purpose are a fertile source of suggestions that would be very valuable for the future use of policy-making bodies.

† It was pointed out by the group that this method is particularly valuable, both with specific problems and in the development of general principles upon which to base action. It is useful with supervisors and, under certain circumstances, employees in general.

Practical Uses	Attendant Benefits
	ticipant has a sense of contributing to group training rather than a sense of receiving only 2. Greater uniformity and better understanding usually result 3. The conference-training method is particularly rich in that it multiplies the sources for ideas
Solving production problems	1. Solutions and decisions are speeded up 2. More individual heads are brought to bear on the problem 3. More factors and wider implications get consideration
In staff and departmental meetings*	1. More active participation by the whole group 2. Better understanding, administration, and performance in the particular area concerned 3. Improvement in teamwork 4. Everyone concerned encouraged to think about the problem under consideration 5. Introduces variety and stimulates interest in such meetings 6. May uncover individual weaknesses in the staff†

By ______________________

Conference Leader

* The group made it clear that they were not thinking of replacing all staff and departmental meetings with formal conferences, nor were they thinking of turning the conducting of all such meetings over to members of the conference-leader group. They were thinking specifically of the executives or other head inviting the conference leader in to a given staff or departmental meeting to achieve certain definite and specific objectives.

† There was some disagreement on this point. Not all of the group felt that the conference was of any special value in this regard. However, it appeared to be the opinion of a significant majority that it would have such a possible benefit to offer.

RECOMMENDATIONS FOR A PLANT CONFERENCE TRAINING PROGRAM

For the guidance of managements that may inaugurate a conference program, and later a plant training program, it should be helpful to present a list of recommendations made to a specific organization that had completed the basic training of its conference leaders.

1. It is recommended that the conference leaders who have completed basic training should be used as a consulting committee to assist the works manager and the supervisor of training in planning the conference program that it is intended to carry on.

2. Since leading conferences, preparing for conferences, and acting as a consulting committee require significant amounts of time, it is recommended that each of the conference leaders be relieved of other duties to the extent that the new work (of preparing for and leading conferences and serving as a consulting committee) will receive their best efforts befitting a major assignment, rather than be crowded aside or slighted by other duties. If certain of these men now have the authority to delegate some of their duties to others or to increase their staff sufficiently, that fact should be drawn to their attention. As an aid in estimating the time required by the participants in the training program it can be pointed out that the preparation for and conducting of one conference, if it is well done, will require 4 hours or more at this stage. Committee work would necessarily be added to this time. Advising and aiding one another will require additional time.

3. In order that the recently acquired skills be not only maintained but improved upon, it is recommended that each conference leader conduct at least two conferences per month, or three in 2 months.

4. It is recommended that each conference leader have the advice of two or three other leaders in the preparation

of his outline for a scheduled conference. Also, it is recommended that one or two other leaders attend his conference and take notes in order to give him constructive and helpful advice regarding his conference techniques. This arrangement should continue for 4 to 6 months.

5. It is a recognized fact that a training program in the making should start conservatively and expand only after the initial program has by its quality and effectiveness proved itself and sold itself to the persons included in the program. These satisfied and enthusiastic persons become salesmen to "enthuse" other persons whom it is planned to include, and the experience gained by those in charge of the program while it is small will enable them to assume the heavier responsibilities of the enlarged program. The program should not be made too large at this early stage. Conferences cannot and should not be used in all training situations. There must be some training that is of an instructor-student nature, such as on-the-job training, apprentice training, etc. And nothing can substitute for the person-to-person intimate discussions between two persons, such as a person and his or her immediate supervisor.

A comprehensive works training program should be planned in which conference programs should play a prominent part, but not the only part. Conferences can aid and be aided by other parts of the training program.

6. It is strongly recommended that a supervisor of training should report directly to the works manager in each case. This is not a criticism of the ability of personnel managers as a group or of any individual personnel manager.

FORMS USEFUL IN THE CONFERENCE PROGRAM

For the use of present and future training directors, several forms are presented for consideration. They will find them useful. Each form has its own introduction.

INFORMATION SHEETS FOR CONFERENCE GROUPS*

Because a great majority of persons do not know the responsibilities of a participant in a conference and do not know his relationship to other participants and to the leader, the form presented is useful in giving them the facts and is recommended for use when a series of conferences is planned.

Objectives of This Conference Series

1. To discuss the problems common to members of this group, and to arrive at possible solutions.
2. To use all of the experience and thinking ability of every member of the group.
3. To promote frank, free, and friendly discussion.

The Job of the Conference Leader

1. To study the problem before discussion, and to prepare a practical outline designed to stimulate full discussion by the conferees.
2. To avoid imposing his own opinion on the group.
3. To guide the discussions, keeping them "on the beam."
4. To record data that should be preserved.
5. To summarize each discussion.
6. To aid in preparation of a report or to prepare a report of the conference.

The Job of Each Conferee

1. To take part in each discussion, to contribute as well as to receive.
2. To be honest, frank, and without prejudice.
3. To avoid taking offense at candid comments of others; to be tolerant; to avoid personalities; to give no intentional offense.
4. To avoid using more than his share of the discussion time; to give every other member adequate opportunity to speak.
5. To accept special assignments if the need arrives.

Not all leaders use an announcement sheet for planned conferences. Many conference participants do not read them in advance or make any preparation before the conference. But if they would make the preparation, the an-

* To be distributed in the first meeting of the series.

nouncement of the coming conference problem would aid them in their preparation and would pay off in terms of better thinking than does extemporaneous thinking in the conference. A sample form is presented below.

TOPIC ANNOUNCEMENT SHEET

(Date of next conference: ____________)

Problem: How can we more successfully use psychology in our daily contacts?

Purposes:

1. To arrive at a better understanding of human nature.
2. To improve one's ability to deal with others.

Definitions: Psychology is the study of human behavior.

Practical psychology is the application of psychological principles to the everyday problems and situations encountered.

Discussion Questions:

1. Why do some persons fail to win your support of their ideas?
2. What should you know before you try to sell an idea to another person?

Sometimes members of a conference group are absent from a scheduled conference. Sometimes it is unavoidable, sometimes the absence was not necessary. It is good psychology to let a person know that his absence was noted. The form presented here has produced good results.

NOTE TO CONFERENCE ABSENTEES

(Name of Conference Series)

To: ____

Department: __________________________________

Your chair was empty at the conference yesterday. You were definitely needed. Was your absence unavoidable? We count on your presence at the next conference.

____

Conference Leader

We do the things we want most to do. The things we do not find time to do really play second fiddle to those other things that we find time to do.

CONFERENCE PROGRAM PROGRESS REPORT

As further evidence that conference programs are being used successfully to aid management at all levels to solve problems and to operate more successfully under today's complex conditions, there follows a report prepared by a steering committee for the plant conference program in one of our major industries. This report is part of the standard practice for that organization, and its contents are of tremendous significance. It is presented as a type of report recommended to maintain records of the progress and results of the conference program.

BI-MONTHLY CONFERENCE REPORT FOR MAY AND JUNE, 1947

The following conferences have been reviewed by the conference leader committee and all recommendations have been put into effect. Therefore, they are to be considered closed.

1. How can we economically decrease the number of different stock sections we use?

2. How can we obtain more efficient truck moves in our _______ department?

> *Comment:* All the recommendations made in this conference have been placed in effect. This was primarily an educational conference and the conferees gained an understanding of how truck moves should be made in the _______ department through this conference.

3. How can the _______ department make better use of job evaluation?

> *Comment:* This conference was conducted at the time that the entire plant was working on job evaluation and wage negotiations. As a result of this conference the foremen of the _______ department have gained a much better understanding of job evaluation and how it should be used.

4. What uniform rules and regulations should be established throughout the plant to assist in obtaining a maximum of productivity?

> *Comment:* This conference was held recently with all foremen and discussed with the department heads. All recommendations

have been referred to top management and a committee has been appointed to outline the policy to be followed by the _______ Works in the future. As far as the conference is concerned, all recommendations have been followed. Future work on this subject will be handled by the committee appointed.

5. What training sessions should be held at _______ Works?

Comment: As the result of this conference a proposed training program has been reviewed with top management, and top management has requested that a training policy be outlined for approval in the very near future. All the recommendations made in this conference have been incorporated in our planned training policy; therefore, we are considering the conference closed.

Following is a list of the open conferences to be followed by the conference leader committee.

1. How can we increase our _______ output?

Comment: The accounting department has been working on recommendations made in this conference. However, considerable work remains to be done.

2. How can we improve our system of obtaining heat-treatment data?

3. Should we install a merit-rating system at _______ Works?

4. Do we need an incentive system at _______ Works?

5. How can we improve our truck service in the _______ department?

Comment: Due to the nature of some of the recommendations made in the above five conferences, these problems will remain open for an indefinite period of time. Considerable work has been done on these problems; however, many recommendations remain open.

6. What can we do to inaugurate a standard-bolt program at _______ Works?

7. What steps should be taken to inaugurate a standard-tubing-size program at our Works?

Comment: The recommendations made in this conference are almost all in effect; however, a little work remains to be done on this subject.

8. How can we more efficiently handle bushings in the machine department?

Comment: Most of the recommendations made in this conference have been put into effect; however, one or two recommendations remain open. This problem will be closed in the near future.

9. How can we improve methods and conditions in the shipping department in the ________ Plant?

Comment: This conference was recently held and the minutes have not been distributed.

10. How can we attain better efficiency and better method in the ________ department?

Comment: This conference was recently held and the minutes have not been distributed.

11. How can the personnel department be more helpful and improve its service to the foremen?

Comment: Most of the recommendations made in this conference were put into effect immediately after the conference was held. Though some work remains to be done, the conference will be closed soon.

12. How can we keep our employees from waiting in line at the clock at quitting time?

Comment: This conference problem was changed to "How can we reduce late starts and early quits in the ________ department?"

Following is a list of open problems to be discussed in conferences at some future date. The problems are not listed in order of their importance. The correct order will be determined by the conference leader committee.

1. What can the foremen do to start the new employee right?
2. Should we revise our tardiness penalty rule?
3. How can we reduce our foot and toe injuries?
4. How can we most effectively use a clearing house for our production at ________ Works?
5. A case-problem conference on the film *The Man in Management.*
6. Should we continue to distribute literature at ________ Works?
7. How can the system of issuing information or instructions be improved so that it will reach all foremen concerned?
8. How can we keep our employees better informed on methods, production, and policies?
9. How can we reduce our hand and finger injuries?

> *Comment:* This conference has been conducted with the ______ department and is scheduled for the ______ department early in June.

10. Should we move the storeroom to the ______ plant warehouse?
11. What are the advantages in having safety equipment in a central location in the plant?
12. Should we discontinue the use of production orders and work to piece numbers at ______ Works?
13. How can the foremen better assist one another?
14. How can the foremen better schedule their time?

> *Comment:* This problem will be discussed and a 35-mm. film on the subject will be shown.

The above problems have been given to the committee by the foremen during the past few months. Following is a list of problems for conferences given to us by the foremen as the result of a request in the foremen's meeting.

1. How can we do a better job of hiring new employees who qualify for jobs that are available?
2. How can we make better use of safety methods?
3. How can we handle face shields in a more orderly manner?
4. How can we more efficiently handle materials in the warehouse to avoid double handling?
5. How can we more effectively identify right- and left-hand materials?

> *Comment:* The foreman who suggested this problem stated that he is referring to ______ and ______ material.

6. How can we more efficiently handle shop rags?
7. How can we keep our move cards clean?
8. How can we get our employees to turn in suggestions that will help production?

The following is a summary of the conference held at ______ Works to date.

Total number of conferences	134
Total conference problems	53
Conference problems closed	41
Conference problems open	12
Conference problems to schedule	23

____
Secretary

Part 3

STATEMENTS AND TYPICAL CONFERENCE REPORTS

CHAPTER 16

THE CONFERENCE PROGRAM IN INDUSTRY

There is a steadily growing number of organizations that are using trained conference leaders to conduct effective conference programs as a part of their integrated plan of factory operation. For the benefit of the great number of organizations that do not yet use a conference program, frank, sincere, and original statements have been prepared by key men whose organizations have adopted the conference plan. Only a few typical statements are reproduced here. However, they do substantiate the author's statements regarding the value of a conference program. The selected statements follow.

THE CONFERENCE PROGRAM AT PERFECT CIRCLE CORPORATION

Beginning in the summer of 1942 the Perfect Circle Corporation for the first time made intensive use of the conference as a training technique. The purpose of these initial conferences was to discover and develop future members of management. In actual practice the program consisted of individual interviews and group conferences under the stimulating direction and guidance of a member of the staff of Purdue University.

Following this preliminary activity, training to develop skilled conference leaders was begun in the Richmond and Hagerstown plants; later a member of management was sent to the Purdue campus for a period of intensive training. During the war the corporation kept from 3 to 10 qualified conference leaders, who conducted hundreds of conferences both of the directed (or teaching) and the open type. Many new types of product and processes were developed during this period and the open-type conference was often extremely valuable in facilitating the exchange of ideas and information. The directed type, however, was more often used. At this period we initiated the system of conducting weekly conferences for supervision and continued that system throughout the emergency. Today, two of the plants continue to use the weekly conferences, and the other two have "called conferences."

The general plan for conferences has undergone some "face lifting," so that at least half of the conferences deal with problems of personnel, and the rest deal with machines, product, processes, or organization. The program is kept so flexible that any current conference topic may be withdrawn and any other topic substituted that the occasion seems to demand. Conferences are carefully planned around topics that are selected by the plant manager or have his approval. Notebook work and textbook work are held to a minimum. Conferences may be directed by a plant manager, personnel manager, or by a specially trained conference leader, but frequently the actual leading is done by a general foreman or a foreman.

The Perfect Circle Corporation has conducted hundreds of conferences, trained many supervisors by that method, believes much good has been derived by such a procedure, and today is making plans for future conferences. We expect to continue solving problems by that method indefinitely.

(Signed) O. M. Aders
Industrial Education Manager
Perfect Circle Corporation

CONFERENCE PROGRAMS IN AMERICAN STEEL FOUNDRIES

Our use of the term "conference" is in the stricter sense set forth by the author. Its planned use is confined to the definition, description, clarification, and solution of problems that fall within the experience or jurisdiction of the majority of the group participating. In our experience, that is a sufficiently wide scope.

Conference leaders are chosen from the line and the staff organizations with the line holding a slight edge in numbers. Their positions range from unit foreman or clerk through department head to assistant works manager.

The success of our program, we believe, stems from what we regard as key factors in its organization and administration. Each works manager appoints one individual to head the conference activity and to handle all the attendant detail. This individual may be a training supervisor, an assistant personnel supervisor in charge of training, an assistant to the works manager, a special engineer, etc., but is always a trained conference leader and is responsible to the works manager for the conference program.

Our works managers have made this program their own. Conference outlines are frequently reviewed by them, before the conference is held, for suggestions they may have to offer. Conference minutes are carefully read by them. Approved conference recommendations requiring action are fed into the line of authority, by the works manager, for action at the level having appropriate authority and responsibility. Any top management rejection or amendment of a conference recommendation is fully explained to the originating group.

Responsibility for follow-up to ensure action is lodged in the line organization by the works manager. The conference leader or the conference-activity head is made responsible for a subsequent summary report to the works manager and the conference group of action taken and results gained. These reports are made bi-monthly or quarterly as each works elects. Every effort is made to see that action takes place as soon after the conference as possible.

Most conference outlines are discussed by a group of conference leaders before taking final form. The conference-leader group serves as a more or less unofficial advisory committee on training and is consulted about many other phases of the works training programs. They are available to any foreman who needs their service.

In the early stages of the program, most of the conference problems came from the conference-leader group and from top management. Soon first- and second-line supervision began to contribute problems and request specific conferences or conference series. At the present time more than 85 per cent of our conferences originate with first- and second-line supervision. Only a little over 10 per cent of the problems are proposed by top operating and staff executives.

A complete file of conference minutes is maintained in our general office by the industrial relations division and a catalogue supplement is issued quarterly. In this way each interested works may obtain a copy of the complete minutes of any conference held at any other works.

Conference minutes are catalogued and cross-indexed under five heads. Company-wide, our total number of conferences have been distributed among these general heads as follows: (1) production programs, 30 per cent; (2) human relations, 25 per cent; (3) training (per se), 15 per cent; (4) administration, 20 per cent; and (5) organization, 10 per cent.

Works managers report several direct benefits from this program. They say that problems are likely to be solved more quickly. Everyone concerned is more certain to be fully informed about the problem and the proposed action because he had an active hand in the solution. Several important dollars-and-cents savings and production improvements have been reported by works managers as direct results of conferences. They report that problems and potential problems are spotted more quickly and, in the main, handled before they become serious.

The various works report indirect benefits that approach the direct benefits in importance and value. They feel that this program has played an important role in increasing the foreman's feeling that he *is* part of management. They report a fine group spirit and cooperative action among the conference-leader group.

We receive many reports of individuals who say that the conference-leader training and experience have helped them greatly in other assignments and activities. Since conference leaders are chosen from among our more alert and promotable men, they are apt to be assigned to increasing responsibilities and special projects. We think that the training and experience of conference leadership contributes to the growth of these individuals.

How to apportion credit between the conference program and other training activities that may have contributed to the improvement of understanding between supervision and workers' representatives, we do not know. We are firmly convinced, however, that the conference program has made an important contribution here. We think of it as another valuable tool in the improvement of labor relations and worker-foreman relations. Some areas of difficulty in these fields have been helped immensely as a direct result of foremen's conferences.

In some places there has been a very gratifying change of attitude and spirit among management representatives that has reflected itself in the whole area of industrial relations. Certainly sole credit cannot be assigned to the conference program, but it did play a part—in some instances a very direct and traceable part.

The conference technique has become one of our most valuable training tools. We do not use it to impart new information as such except as the less experienced or talented foremen gain and learn by sharing experiences and ideas with older or wiser heads. We do use it intensively to work out mutually acceptable practical applications of new information that was originally imparted by lecture, exposition, etc.

Perhaps the greatest training contributions of the conference technique have been made as a device to (1) uncover needs for training, (2) uncover or stimulate a desire for needed training, (3) work out with those concerned the content, method, etc., of such proposed training activities, and (4) work out subsequent practical applications of the knowledge, skills, etc., contributed by other training activities.

Through the conference device, we believe that we have saved much lost motion, trial and error, and general dissatisfaction in our other training activities.

The operating division head, works managers who have used it, the manager of industrial relations, and the company's training supervisor are unanimous in their feeling that we would not give up our conference program under any set of circumstances that we can foresee. Our people regard it as a ready aid that is freely available to any level of management at any time. We have come to look upon our corps of conference leaders as a rich management resource and upon the conference technique and program as an indispensable management tool.

(Signed) E. J. Walsh
Manager of Industrial Relations
American Steel Foundries

THE CONFERENCE PROGRAM AT UNITED STATES RUBBER COMPANY, MISHAWAKA, IND.

For 10 years the Mishawaka Plant of the United States Rubber Company has used a conference program as a part of the plant-wide training program. The conference program has been useful in conveying information through all levels of management. The information consists of instructions, educational topics, problem solutions, and miscellaneous material involving the rapid factual and efficient information to all management representatives. Foremen have learned to conduct regularly scheduled meetings with their supervisors, assistant foremen, and promotion prospects.

As a result of conference-leader training, the superintendents' meetings have been more effective in that two-way conversation has been established by and between superintendents and key foremen. Individual performance of many key men has noticeably improved since it has afforded key people with ability and opportunity to express their ability and capacity in the general operation of the business. Indeed such cases undoubtedly augment the general educational program that is constantly being operated by the plant training director.

(Signed) F. A. Miller
Manager, Industrial Relations
United States Rubber Company
Mishawaka, Ind.

THE CONFERENCE PROGRAM AT AMERICAN MAIZE-PRODUCTS COMPANY, ROBY, IND.

The conference program has for several years been the backbone of our training efforts. Through the program, our top management was able to convince our foremen that they are definitely a part of management. Our management, from the vice-president down, participated. We found it was a good arrangement. The sincere interest of management in the program was proved.

We were able to organize a policy- and standard-practices manual through the conferences. The value of this can readily be seen when you realize that the foremen felt they were actually formulating policy.

At present we are planning for a bigger and better plant training program. The conference program will continue to be the most important part of the total efforts. Additional conference leaders will be needed and will receive the same basic intensive training that was received by the first group with such good results.

(Signed) T. G. Higgins
Industrial Relations Manager
Roby, Ind.

THE CONFERENCE PROGRAM AT CONTINENTAL FOUNDRY AND MACHINE COMPANY

In carrying on our program of supervisory conferences we found it very advantageous to make use of the services offered by Purdue University. Professor Stigers conducted a number of general conferences and then gave conference-leader training to a carefully selected group of supervisors. These leaders then proceeded to conduct conferences already closely related to the supervisory problems of our plant.

We are planning to carry on with the program because we have been satisfied as to the real benefits both to the company and to the supervisors. Perhaps the most significant of these benefits were as follows:

Working out the solution of problems involving production, safety, labor turnover, etc., by drawing on the combined experience of the various supervisors.

Uncovering so-called supervisory "gripes," which might not have come to light in any other way. (Supervisors are human—and have their own grievances just as rank-and-file workers do.)

Developing leadership ability and poise among those who were trained to conduct conferences.

Acquainting individual supervisors with the problems of their fellow supervisors with the result that better understanding and close cooperation have been developed.

While the entire program has been our own and under our control, we have had the advantage and the advice and assistance of Professor Stigers, who has at all times worked closely with our own supervisor of training, J. D. Holtzapple.

(Signed) W. J. Hebard
Personnel Director
East Chicago, Ind.

THE CONFERENCE PROGRAM AT CONTINENTAL STEEL CORPORATION, KOKOMO, IND.

Our program has grown from a small beginning. Several men attended a night-school program of training conferences. Later, one individual attended an intensive conference-leader training course. Since that time, 150 of our management personnel have been given conference training. Sixty-five of this number, whose duty it would be to conduct departmental conferences, were trained as leaders. The remainder of the group were given training mainly to familiarize them with the conference method. We had found that conferences proceeded more rapidly and were less inclined to stray from the discussion topic when the conferees understood the method being followed. We did not require members of the latter group to lead a conference, but many of them volunteered to do so. During these conferences many general and specific plant problems were discussed. Some of the men took this opportunity to get some "gripes" out of their systems, and most of them realized for the first time that they were a part of management, with its many duties and responsibilities.

Solutions of the conference problems were reached largely by the exchange of information between the conferees. Company staff specialists were called in when topics included specific subjects outside the range of knowledge of the group members.

Now for a few practical benefits growing out of our conferences:

One of our division superintendents believed that an excessive amount of grease was being used in one of his departments. He called a conference of all those concerned with the use of the grease, and by putting into practice the information and ideas obtained from the conferees, he was able to make savings in excess of 50 per cent. For example, grease consumption for the month previous to the conference was 50,850 pounds. For the month following the conference, 24,775 pounds of grease were used, a reduction of 26,075 pounds or 51.27 per cent.

Another supervisor held a conference to discuss roll breakage. As a result he was able to reduce this loss well over 50 per cent.

Mechanical, electrical, and other production delays have been greatly reduced through the use of conferences. These conferences included supervisors from both production and service departments, and the discussions led to better planning and coordination of effort. Furthermore, as a result of the elimination of the production delays, the morale of the production workers was greatly improved.

One of our superintendents says that training in conference leading has enabled him to more intelligently conduct other types of departmental meetings, largely because timidity has been replaced by a feeling of self-confidence. This training, plus participation in conferences by the foremen in his department, has made them more cooperative, due to their better understanding of the problems involved. One outstanding case related to one of his foremen who had been in the department for several years. This foreman would assume only the responsibility that he could not dodge. During his conference-training practice period he listened to discussion by more progressive foremen, which so stimulated his own thinking that he now assumes more of the authority and responsibility inherent in his job, thus increasing his value to himself, his superintendent, and his company.

In our stores department certain practices that reduced the efficiency of the department had gradually developed over a period of time. The chief storekeeper held a conference of all stores department employees, in which these practices were discussed, in order to obtain practical suggestions for the correction of these inefficient practices and also to suggest other improvements. As a result, several practical suggestions were made and adopted with good results. A general understanding was also reached regarding the duties and responsibilities of each member of the stores department.

The information brought out in this conference pointed out the need for a conference with a group composed of department heads and their assistants. The conference was conducted by the chief storekeeper, who explained in detail the changes in practice and pointed out in some detail the correct manner of writing stores requisitions and the rules to be followed in so doing. This meeting brought about the necessity for

1. The clarification of certain items in the code book, to be made by the cost department.

2. The need for foreman training in writing stores requisitions.

As a result of these conferences, we believe that in each department the morale has improved: departmental policies have been discussed and formulated, supervisory responsibilities have been made clear and authority delegated, points of strength and weakness of foremen have been uncovered, efforts have been coordinated, operating and personnel problems have been solved, a definite line organization has been established, and each level or authority is better respected and supported.

The workers are more intelligently supervised, they understand and respect the foremen's authority, and many small problems are solved before they have a chance to grow. As a result of our many conferences, new and practical ideas are being submitted by the workers and many have been adopted.

(Signed) R. C. Owen
Training Director
Kokomo, Ind.

THE CONFERENCE PROGRAM AT THE HARRISON STEEL CASTINGS, ATTICA, IND.

In the fall of 1946, this plant initiated a conference-training program for foremen. Our main objectives were four: (1) To show the importance and value of human engineering, (2) to instruct the foremen in modern industrial practices and theories, (3) to consider various tasks of a foreman and to discuss ways and means of getting the tasks accomplished in the best practical manner, (4) to stimulate the foremen to do constructive thinking.

We attempted to achieve objective 1 by having conferences entitled "Leadership qualities" and "Should foremen make 'howdy' rounds each morning" and analyzing case problems in human relations. Objective 2 was handled by the use of semicontrolled conferences on such subjects as time and motion study, job evaluation, job analysis, merit rating, and economics. Economics were stressed all through the conference series. Discussions concerning supply and demand, why men work, prices, interest, etc., were lively and very important. To achieve objective 3, we first considered the job of a foreman generally, and then specifically held conferences on various phases, such as "How can we reduce accident proneness?" "How can we improve our planning?" "How can we reduce wastage of supplies?" "How can we reduce wastage of manpower?" How can we improve our methods of job instruction?" etc. In fulfilling our fourth and final objective, we relied on case problems and supervisory quizzes.

We feel sure that this method of training is a very definite step forward, compared to the lecture method, but definite results are very hard to point out except in the case of foreman morale, which we can measure and state definitely that an improvement has been noted.

(Signed) Francis A. Shoaf
Director of Training
Attica, Ind.

BENEFIT TO INDIVIDUALS

Evidence has been offered showing how organizations profit by using a conference program. There is also great value to the individuals who learn to lead conferences and to participate in conferences. A few short statements illustrate this point.

"This conference-leadership training has been worth at least $1500 to me."

"This course is really as valuable as a full year in a university."

"I was skeptical in the beginning. Now I can't tell you how glad I am that you persuaded me to take this course in conference leadership."

"These conferences have done a lot for us foremen. Now we know what goes on and why. And we know one another better. I'm definitely happier than I was this time last year, due to these conferences."

A superintendent states: "The individuals who attend conferences and who receive conference reports hand in better reports to me on those assignments in which I require a report. I know they are better men because of our conference program."

CONFERENCE PROGRAM IN SCHOOL ORGANIZATIONS

It has been pointed out that a conference program can and should be used in school organizations as well as in manufacturing organizations. In a few centers the idea is catching on. There will be more. For the encouragement of school administrators who wish to use a modern and very effective tool, there are presented two statements from school administrators who do use and believe in them.

THE USE OF A CONFERENCE PROGRAM AND CONFERENCE LEADERSHIP TRAINING IN PUBLIC SCHOOLS

During the many years that I have been promoting, sponsoring, and scheduling the training of conference leaders for business and industry, I have always felt the need of such training in the public schools, the educational field. The initial tryout consisted of a series of conferences led by a trained conference leader (Prof. M. F. Stigers), using public-school supervisors and principals as participants in analyzing and solving administrative policies and problems. This series proved very conclusively that we must train some of our administrators, if not all of them, so that they can lead conferences with the principals-and-supervisors group and also with teachers in the separate buildings. These administrator conference leaders are also used to lead conferences with teachers in the subject-matter fields as well as other curriculum work.

The functional utility of conferences in departmentalized schools, such as high schools, technical high schools, and vocational schools, makes it imperative that industrial, distributive occupations, and curriculum coordinators be trained as leaders. Selected teachers, especially department heads in the larger schools, can and should use conference methods and should also be available for part-time employment as conference directors with small businesses, industries, and labor organizations.

(Signed) Fred E. Benson
Director of Hammond Technical Vocational High School
City of Hammond
Hammond, Ind.

CONFERENCE TECHNIQUE AS A METHOD OF ADMINISTRATION

Schools can be administered, generally speaking, in three ways. The old school was administered in a rather autocratic fashion by one man, the superintendent of schools. Later, superintendents saw the wisdom of sharing the making of policies and decisions, and gradually invited several members of the administrative staff to discuss problems with them. Today, more and more superintendents are drawing upon the personnel of their entire staff for ideas and for making decisions concerning the operation of the school program. This tendency is wholly desirable and in harmony with democratic administration in a democratic society.

One of the techniques in bringing about participation of staff personnel and capitalizing upon their ideas is to arrange for a series of conferences on topics upon which the staff members may or should be interested. Conferences, however, are not likely to be too successful unless they are directed by a person with experience and, still better, by a person who has been trained in conference techniques.

Too little thought has been given to successful techniques in both the individual conference and the group conference. If such conferences are to be successful, the personnel should be properly selected and the agenda should be carefully prepared and properly organized with relation to background, presenting of the problem, creating ideas, and closing, with the individuals of the group wanting to proceed with the project or to use their influence against it. Besides, the conference leader needs to know how to direct the questions to stimulate thinking and arouse constructive thought. Also he needs to know how to promote confidence in the other fellow, get him to talk, and not dominate the conference with his own speaking and thinking.

The conference technique brings forth many ideas that otherwise would be lost. Further, it promotes participation and prepares staff personnel to live democratically. It promotes a feeling of belongingness which enhances desirable staff morale. Not the least of the outcome is sharing in the success of the venture or in the responsibility for its failure.

(Signed) Harold H. Church
Superintendent of Schools
Elkhart, Ind.

CHAPTER 17

SELECTED CONFERENCE REPORTS

The selected conference reports in this unit are included for two primary reasons. First, they accurately represent the variety of problems profitably discussed in industrial and school organizations. Second, they are valuable in that they present the thinking of men and women who fill important positions in schools and in industry. The ideas and thinking recorded in these conference reports are helpful source materials for conference-leader trainers, for conference leaders, and for all members of the executive family. They can be of help in shaping policies and in solving work problems of many kinds. Both the foreman who plans to conduct conferences with his production workers and the works manager who conducts staff meetings can find helpful ideas in these conference reports. Likewise, in school organizations, superintendents, principals, and teachers can ascertain how other school groups have approached important problems. The comparatively few reports presented in this text should show how valuable would be a library of hundreds of conference reports on a wide range of problems. The author of this text has found his own library of conference reports of great help in his work, and it has served many other persons to whom it has been made available. The building up of such a library is recommended to both school and industrial organizations.

MANAGEMENT CONFERENCE SERIES
CONFERENCE REPORT

Nov. 5, 1947

Problem: What kinds of information do industrial employees need in order better to understand their responsibilities and opportunities as industrial workers?

Objectives:

1. To list the kinds of information that would help to build this understanding.

2. To select from the preceding list the few that should be used as a beginning.

3. To discuss and then to recommend who should present this information.

4. To discuss and then to recommend how it should be done.

Definition: The term "industrial employees" is arbitrarily limited to employees below the level of foreman or department head, persons who have no managerial responsibility.

Opening Statement: Frequently I have heard factory workers speak disparagingly and even bitterly of their company or of the top management of their company. Their comments prove lack of confidence and lack of respect. Sometimes there is a temptation to express their feelings in some form of violence. I have heard comments such as, "I wouldn't work here another day if I could get another job that paid enough to live on"; or, "Look at that high-hat —— the old robber!"

This attitude of lack of confidence, this feeling of getting a raw deal, and this resentment are costly to our national industry. Even a mild case of this sort of thing slows down a worker, takes his mind from his work, impairs his efficiency and his value as an employee.

What is wrong with this statement: "I'm being paid $1

an hour, I'll do $1 worth of work"? What is wrong about workers opposing improved and more efficient methods of production?

No organization has ever displayed a 100 per cent perfect example of teamwork and efficiency. A few do quite well, but these are far from perfect. The national average of industrial efficiency actually attained has never exceeded 65 per cent of what could have been accomplished; and today productivity per worker is in many cases less than in 1940. *Why?*

If there were complete confidence between workers and management, based upon a full and complete understanding of many things not now known or understood by workers generally, we could achieve a standard of production and therefore a standard of living that exist now only in dreams. And there would be job happiness and peace of mind to replace fear, distrust, and envy.

What are the things workers need to know that would make them see both their responsibilities and opportunities as workers in American industry? I believe the problem can be solved. If it is not, the alternative will be increasingly costly.

Discussion: The discussion group agreed with the leader that the problem as stated constitutes a real challenge and demands sound thinking and constructive action. In the initial discussion the definition of the term "industrial employee" was accepted. The objectives were taken up in the order listed.

For objective 1, the following list was made:

1. Company history and background.
2. Economic costs of being absent.
3. Product information.

   a. What our products are.
   b. Who our customers are.
   c. How our product is used.
   d. Who our competitors are.

4. How much work an employee should do to constitute a fair day's work.
5. Worker benefits.
   a. Insurance.
   b. Hospitalization, etc.
6. Organization chart for the works.
   a. Include the worker's own job, to whom he reports, and his responsibility and authority.
7. Company policy with reasons and needed interpretations.
8. Services offered by the various departments.
9. How rates and time standards are arrived at.
10. The reason his job exists; *i.e.,* the importance of it.
11. Show how improved methods do not endanger jobs.
12. Benefits of the suggestion system.
13. Certainty of later rewards for honest effort.
14. Social functions sponsored by the athletic association.
15. Data on costs and sales.
16. The rewards of working safely.
17. Modern industrial economics.
    a. Productivity and prices.
    b. The worker's relation to productivity and price.
    c. Cost of scrap.
    d. How improved methods reduce cost.
    e. Miscellaneous costs.
    f. Proof that management salaries are earned.
18. Tell workers how well they are doing, constructive help to do better, and praise for good work.

Turning to objective 2, the conferees selected from the preceding list the few that should be used as a beginning.

1. Company history, policies, safety rules, services of departments, and employee benefits.
2. Quantity and quality of work, how rates and time standards are established.

3. Modern industrial economics.

Turning to objective 3, the conferees determined who should present these information items. Item 1 above should be presented by management through the personnel department. Item 2 should be presented by management through trained foremen. Item 3 was given three alternatives:

a. By management through the training department and trained foremen.
b. By a training institution, such as Purdue University, the University of Chicago, or Northwestern University.
c. Through the Department of Labor, with the cooperation of labor unions.

The conference group favored the Department of Labor proposal, except for the probable delay in getting started. It was suggested that the Department of Labor could appoint an institution (such as Purdue University) to carry on this project. The idea of having the Department of Labor or a university present this industrial economics was to avoid suspicion by workers that management had an ulterior motive.

Turning to objective 4, the conferees determined how the items of information should be presented. The first item of the three selected should be presented to groups of new employees by a trained person (probably using booklets and other printed matter as aids). The second item should be presented by a combination of person-to-person talks between foreman and worker, and worker conferences conducted by the foreman. The third item should be presented by means of group meetings of not over 50 employees at a time, meeting on company property. Part or all of the expense involved should be met by management (for the employer).

Conclusion: The conference group reviewed its recommendations as outlined above and reaffirmed them.

The group recommends that management seriously consider the recommendations and hopes that steps will be taken to put them into effect. Individually the group pledged themselves to cooperate fully in such a program.

By ______________________
Conference Leader

MANAGEMENT CONFERENCE SERIES
CONFERENCE REPORT

Jan. 25, 1946

Problem: How can we reduce maintenance cost and the production delays caused by unexpected breakdowns?

Objectives:

1. To identify the preventable causes that bring about premature breakdowns.

2. To discuss and recommend a plan to reduce maintenance cost and the production delays caused by unexpected breakdowns.

Opening Statement: We are meeting here today to discuss a problem becoming more and more acute, "How can we reduce maintenance cost, and, also, how can we reduce production delays caused by unexpected breakdowns?" Production delays caused by premature and unexpected breakdowns run parallel to high maintenance cost.

There are probably many ways by which we can increase production efficiency and lower the operating cost. In this discussion we will limit ourselves to ways and means by which we can reduce production delays that are caused by unexpected breakdowns, and also ways and means to reduce maintenance cost. When a premature and unexpected breakdown occurs, it not only means premature costly repairs, but also the loss of valuable production time. Men and machines stand idle.

The full advantages of a good preventive maintenance system are not yet fully appreciated by all. Some do not understand what preventive maintenance really means. Others believe that it is an expensive and complicated procedure. You will find those who will say, "Yes, that's fine business for the other fellow, but it will never work here," or "We have no need for it at this plant."

To reestablish some facts in your mind, let us look at the

statements written on the board: "Maintenance is the proper use and upkeep of equipment so as to obtain maximum efficiency and longest life. The purpose of practicing preventive maintenance is to prevent unnecessary breakdowns, delays, and premature costly repairs."

Men, this is not going to be just another meeting. I need full cooperation from every one of you. We will try to arrive at a definite conclusion with some concrete recommendations so that real action can be taken. Let us approach this problem with an open mind. We are not gathered here to point an accusing finger at anyone. Let us deal in reality and see if we can solve this problem.

Discussion: In pursuance of the first objective, the leader asked this question, "What are some of the *preventable causes* that bring about premature breakdowns?" In response the group offered the following list:

1. *Abuse of equipment.* The group felt that this was quite a broad statement but that it should remain listed because of its extreme importance.

2. *Improper greasing and oiling.* Consensus of the group pointed to the fact that even though this is listed it isn't a very great contributing factor to high maintenance and production delays in our plant.

3. *Inadequate inspection.* A question was asked, "Inadequate inspection by whom?" A discussion here brought out the fact that both the inspection department supervisors and the production supervisors were quite negligent.

4. *Improper training.* The group expressed its opinion that in an over-all picture there can be definite improvement in our methods of on-the-job training. It was also expressed that we were lax in proper follow-up.

5. *Lack of proper operator attitude.* The above statement refers to the careless attitude that many machine operators have developed. They are not concerned whether machines are in good condition or not, or whether work turned out is of good quality.

6. *Lack of foresight.* The ability to judge when repairs are necessary and to foresee how extensive the repairs might get to be if the machine is kept in operation (production vs. repair).

7. *Inadequate replacement of worn-out equipment.* The group felt that the old and obsolete equipment had a definite bearing on high maintenance cost and production delays.

8. *Inadequate replacement of worn-out parts.*

9. *Lack of full appreciation of value of equipment.* The group commented that supervisors didn't fully appreciate their responsibility toward the equipment in their department.

10. *Improper equipment layout.* Referring here to space allotment. The fact that it is difficult to make repairs in close spaces.

11. *Inadequate supply of replacement parts.* The fact that some improvement can be made in maintaining proper replacements. It must not be overemphasized because it would be economically foolish to stock every part that can possibly fail.

12. *Failure to report breakdowns promptly.* Also failure to report obvious anticipated breakdowns.

13. *Overloading of equipment.*

In approach to the second objective, the group reviewed the list and pointed out those points that were the greatest contributors toward high maintenance cost and delays. These were items 1, 3, 4, 5, 7, and 13.

To further the second objective, the leader asked the following question: "What can be done *to correct* these faults?" The discussion that followed brought forth this list:

1. A daily departmental maintenance log to be maintained. It was the opinion of the group that if some sort of daily log were maintained by the departmental supervisors, showing what mechanical breakdowns or delays

transpired throughout the day, proper analysis could be made therefrom and proper corrective steps could be taken.

2. A review of principles of job-instruction training to be given at the departmental meetings.

3. Conferences on abuse of equipment should be held. The group indicated that it might be beneficial to hold a series of conferences on abuse of equipment.

4. Different methods of practicing preventive methods to be studied. Literature to be supplied to the supervisors on the subject of preventive maintenance and, if possible, trips be made to other plants where a good practice of preventive maintenance has been established.

Conclusion: It is apparent from the preceding discussion that much can be done. Machinery should be set up so that we can obtain definite action.

The conference group recommends that management appoint a well-represented committee to study and present a definite and practical method of keeping a running log of the important equipment in the plant. This log is not only to supply information of repairs made but also needed repairs to be made and is to be recorded in such a manner that it can be of benefit to the operating department as well as to the maintenance department.

That group recommends that a copy of this report be submitted to all department heads and, if possible, to all supervisors.

The group recommends that the department heads devote a portion of their meeting at regular intervals, as they see fit, to a review of the principles of job-instruction training.

The group also requests that selected supervisors be given the opportunity to visit other plants (plants that have established a good practice of preventive maintenance) to study their methods.

By ______________________

Conference Leader

MANAGEMENT CONFERENCE SERIES
CONFERENCE REPORT

Dec. 20, 1945

Problem: "How can we improve our cooperative engineering program?"

Objectives:

1. To understand the general nature of the plan.
2. To discuss difficulties, errors, and weaknesses encountered in its previous operation.
3. To discuss and recommend steps that may improve the plan.

Opening Statement: I have asked an opportunity to discuss with you, "How can we improve our cooperative engineering training program?" because it has suddenly become a current "hot" problem. Young men who may be interested in and qualified for such a program are gradually becoming available to industry again. Some returning servicemen are going to want to take advantage of the provisions for training offered in so-called "G.I. Legislation." A split work-study program will appeal to many of these men more than an all-study program. The state university, which cooperated with this organization before the war, is getting ready to take care of the boys who want or need the cooperative type of program. Our own management is planning to seize this opportunity to locate and train talented men for the good of our own organization. Your local management has recently had a letter from the operating vice-president requesting them to take steps to select some cooperative trainees to be ready for entry with the semester that will begin in March. Our president is personally very much interested in our continuing to participate in this plan.

What I am saying "boils down" to this: Somebody has to begin now to plan ways and means of setting up this program so that our works and the entire corporation, and the trainees can each get the maximum benefit out of this cooperative education project.

So far as this works is concerned, it seems to me that the group here in this room, because of your previous experience with this plan, certainly ought to be able to make suggestions and recommendations that will bear great weight with company officials and that will be helpful to other works with less experience.

Discussion: Suppose we look at our first objective, "To understand the general nature of the plan." You will see here on the center panel a very sketchy outline of the major features of the plan.

You will note:

1. Cooperative selection of trainees by school and industry on the basis of

   a. Previous school record
   b. Tests of aptitude, interest, and intelligence
   c. Interviews, references, etc.

2. Alternate, 17-week semesters of work and study over 5-year course

   Comment: Previously, trainees alternated every 8 weeks.

3. Work schedule planned to give wide and well-rounded shop experience

   a. First 3 years largely confined to department of major interest
   b. Last 2 years involving short periods in other major departments

4. Trainees on a progressive sliding salary scale.

It would hardly be profitable at this stage to get into a discussion on the merits of various work plans or on the question of salary. Other than that, does anyone have any question about the broad features of the plan? (No major questions were raised at this point.)

If there are no further questions, let me ask, "Do any of you remember or think of any difficulties we encountered in the previous operation of this plan? Did we, in your opinion, make any mistakes? Were there any weaknesses in the program?"

The following list was developed by the group in response to these questions.

1. Salary too low.

   Comment: The group indicated that during the early operation of the plan the shop earnings fell too far short of meeting subsistence requirements while in school. There was some further indication that the group felt that in at least the early stages of previous operation of this plan there had been a lack of a clear and definite policy.

2. Lack of sufficient thought in selection.

   Comment: The group indicated that selection during the previous operation of the plan had taken too little account of the expressed interests and the measured interests (interest tests) of trainees in specific lines of work. The group further expressed the feeling that the previous selection had paid too little attention to the width of the gap between the trainee's previous schooling and his beginning of the cooperative apprentice program. They felt that some few individuals who had been out of school several years had great difficulty with the program and dropped out, not because of a lack of interest or willingness to work or ability, but because the long period that had elapsed during which they were not used to study caused them to get a very bad start during their first semester in school and thus handicapped them severely in the program.

3. The group felt that there had not been sufficiently close coordination between the school and the local plant and company in planning individual curricula.

4. It was suggested that not enough detailed planning had been done for the development of trainees in the shop departments.

5. It was forcibly brought out that the group felt that department heads and immediate supervisors had not been given enough help and guidance in planning for (*a*) the effective use of and (*b*) the development of trainees in their departments and units.

> *Comment:* Referring to items 4 and 5, these comments apply both to the department of major assignment and to the departments in which short-term assignments were given to broaden the trainee's experience.

6. It was felt that the previous plan did not always afford sufficiently wide experience.

> *Comment:* It was felt by the group that all trainees in this program should have some time in the home office engineering department and in the plant. It appeared to be the consensus that trainees attached to the home office engineering department should receive considerable shop experience and that trainees attached to one of the plants should receive considerable home office engineering department experience. It was recognized that the latter experience would necessarily be less extensive because of the number of trainees we would have to provide for.

7. It was felt that a definite weakness in the previous plan arose out of failure to sufficiently explain and sell supervisors and department heads on the features and merits of this plan.

> *Comment:* It was brought out that at least a few supervisors who had had trainees assigned to them

had feared that they would be pushed out of a job by the man they were being asked to train.

8. The group believed that the trainees had in some cases not been made to understand clearly their position, prospects, etc.

9. The group felt that in some cases emergencies of one kind or another had been allowed to interfere with this training program to an unnecessary degree.

10. In the beginning of this program during its former operation, the group believed that trainees had not been shown clearly enough how much money they would have to have in order to meet the expenses of this program.

> *Comment:* It was brought out that several people who showed great promise had been forced to drop out because they could not finance their portion of the program.

11. The group was of the opinion that placing the trainee in his department of major assignment or interest during the first 3 years of the program and devoting the last 2 years to general experience in various departments was a reverse approach to the problem and had been a weakness during the previous operation of the program.

12. The group believed that the program had not been sufficiently explained to all employees during its previous operation.

13. The group felt that not enough thought had been given to providing for deserving and ambitious, but financially embarrassed, employees who were interested in the program but were unable to finance it.

> *Comment:* Considerable discussion arose on this point and the feeling of the group was pretty well unanimous. However, neither here nor later in the conference were we able to develop any constructive suggestion as to how management might handle this problem.

The leader indicated that this appeared to be a fruitful list upon which to proceed. It seemed to represent most of the major points upon which the group felt we needed to work. No additional weaknesses were offered.

The leader then asked the following question: "Getting right down to brass tacks, what can we recommend that management actually do to make our new plan stronger or better or more profitable than our previous plan?" This question resulted in the development of the following list of "Things to Do":

1. Former cooperative apprentice graduates now in the shop should be consulted in the revival of and the administration of the cooperative apprentice training program.

> *Comment:* It was very clearly the feeling of the group that the objective they had in mind here was not to magnify the importance of such graduates, but rather to encourage management to take advantage of the experiences upon which these men could draw to be helpful to management and new trainees.

2. Some means should be devised through which graduate cooperative apprentices now in the shop could serve as counselors to trainees and prospective trainees.

3. Provisions should be made to publicize and explain the complete details of the cooperative apprentice plan to our employees. On this basis employees who are interested or who have members of their family who are interested should be encouraged to investigate and volunteer as candidates for enrollment.

4. It was emphasized by the group that management should make every possible provision to give department heads and the immediate supervisors under whom trainees work every possible help and guidance in fulfilling their obligations and duties under this program.

5. The group recommended that management plan the cooperative apprentice program in such a way that the trainee spend his first 3 years getting general experience in all of the departments of the plant and his last 2 years

specializing in the department of his major assignment or interest.

> *Comment:* It was implied that this would include home office engineering department experience for the shop trainees and shop experience for the home office engineering department trainees.

Conclusion: The leader summarized at this point as follows: "We have pointed out what appeared to most of this group to be flaws in the operation of our previous plan. We have suggested a number of things that we think will result in improvements if they are adopted. It is recognized that these suggestions generally will be minor changes in the over-all training program. Evidently it is the feeling of this group that the previous program was, in general, very well planned and very well executed. But we do feel that we have been helpful to management in its efforts to improve this training program.

"Now, are we done? Can we quit where we are right now, or do we need to set up some machinery to get consideration of our recommendations under way?"

The conference group instructed the leader to include as part of the minutes the following instructions: The works training supervisor shall submit the recommendations of the group embodied in these minutes to management through his regular channels of report. Through these same channels he shall request that management submit and recommend to the general office those suggestions which appear to be practical, encouraging, and supporting their adoption. He shall be responsible to the group for securing consideration of these recommendations through the channels normally open to him and shall report back to the group at a later date the results of his efforts. He shall, if possible, secure information from management regarding their action on these suggestions and report to the group.

By ______________________

Conference Leader

MANAGEMENT CONFERENCE SERIES
CONFERENCE REPORT

Feb. 7, 1946

Problem: How can we reduce plant accidents?

Objectives:

1. To identify the underlying causes of plant accidents.
2. To suggest what we can do at this plant in order to reduce the most important causes.

Opening Statement: The prevention of accidents is an important subject in every industrial plant. Accident prevention is largely a matter of cooperation, instructions, and follow-up.

It can easily be realized that whenever people gather and use machinery, the possibility of accidents increases. A person must not only watch what he is doing but must also keep a watch on his fellow worker.

The importance and magnitude of the problem can best be brought out by the use of figures. Casualties on the war front from the start to V-J Day were 261,608 killed and 651,911 wounded. During this same period on the home front 355,000 were killed and 36,000,000 were injured, and of these over 1¼ million were permanent injuries. The accident toll at work alone was 160,000 killed and 15,000,000 injured. Our plant so far for the months of October, November, and December had a total of 8,928 hours lost due to injuries.

When you figure that practically every plant accident incurs some expense, the problem is really great. This expense may be in the form of lost time, loss of production, loss of income, or expensive compensation.

From these statements it can be seen that management has a big problem and responsibility in seeing that safety is observed to the fullest extent.

Discussion: The leader pointed out that the discussion

was intended to accomplish the two tasks as outlined on the board. The first objective was developed through the leader asking the group to list the underlying causes of plant accidents in general.

1. *Poor housekeeping.* It was a definite belief that a messy or dirty and unkept plant is conducive to a high accident rate.

2. *Horseplay.*

3. *Improper handling of equipment.* Subjects and examples included in this discussion were flasks, castings, materials, tools, gas, electricity, etc.

4. *Lack of proper clothing.* This refers to improper shoes, sleeves, head coverings, etc.

5. *Haste (taking chances).* Oftentimes a job will be done the quickest way although it may not be the safe way. Running of lift trucks at high speeds and handling of cranes and other moving equipment.

6. *Improper instructions.* Unless a person is trained properly as to how to perform his work, there are many possibilities of accidents to both himself and others.

7. *Overloading of chains.* It was felt this was a definite possibility in that chains are not handled correctly.

8. *Faulty equipment.*

9. *Not using provided safety equipment.*

10. *Not following instructions.*

11. *Not reporting lack of safety guards.* A worker or supervisor should have enough interest in his work to try to see that all the equipment he comes in contact with is in satisfactory condition.

12. *Improper maintenance.* It was felt that oftentimes after equipment is repaired the maintenance men do not replace safety devices that were removed during the repairing operation.

13. *Poor working conditions.* It was felt that dark areas, cold areas, or smoky areas could be definite causes of accidents.

14. *Use of improper tools.* It was brought out that at times the use of wrong tools can cause accidents.

15. *Poor physical and mental conditions.* A person should be in good physical condition to work around moving equipment and a person must keep his mind on his work while in a shop. He cannot daydream.

16. *Improper use of compressed air.* This air must not be used for cleaning of clothing.

17. *Drinking of intoxicating liquors.* This can cause very serious accidents in a plant where mechanical equipment is in use.

18. *Lack of teamwork.* Without the proper enthusiasm of a worker or foreman for his job, he may be a hazard to both himself and his fellow worker. Groups must work together as a unit.

19. *Too crowded conditions.* It was brought out that although areas are kept clean and in order, if stocks are piled high because of lack of room, accidents could easily happen.

20. *Lack of protective fire equipment.*

21. *Lazy workers.* This refers to workers who leave tools and other articles lie around; also it refers to uninterested workers.

22. *Lack of follow-up.* A follow-up by the working supervisor and safety inspector is necessary.

23. *Lack of well-rounded-out safety program.* A good program should include safety group meetings, awards, use of posters and pictures, definite set policy and definite reprimands.

24. *Lack of enforcement of safety rules.*

25. *Poor example set by key men.* Oftentimes top men do not set a good example for their workers.

26. *Indifference to possible accidents.* A person may have worked on a job so long that operations become mechanical with but little regard for safety.

27. *Failure to heed or use warning signals.*

The leader then asked the group, in order to complete the second objective, to check the causes they felt were the most important. The group selected eight, which were as follows:

1. Poor housekeeping.
2. Horseplay.
6. Improper instructions.
8. Faulty equipment.
13. Poor working conditions.
23. Lack of well-rounded-out safety program.
24. Lack of enforcement of safety rules.
25. Poor example set by key men.

The group then made the following recommendations:

1. Have photographs made of actual hazardous conditions in the shop and display them on the various department bulletin boards.
2. Have better safety policy established.
3. More authority delegated to safety personnel.
4. More frequent safety inspection.
5. Better check and study of each accident.
6. Supervisors to enforce rules.
7. Establish some type of reward system by department.
8. Make better use of National Safety Council training and programs.
9. Have meetings that will include safety inspector, foreman, and worker.
10. Have worker appointed as monitor to assist in safety program. He would help the supervisor take care of his area.
11. Must have satisfactory reprimand program including penalties.
12. To follow through with regular organization lines, but with safety inspector having final say.

Conclusion: The conferees were asked to aid in suggesting ways and means of making the recommendations effective.

The persons or departments having authority to take action were named for each item as follows:

1. Safety department.
2. Top management, aided by all other management persons, including the safety director and his staff.
3. Top management.
4. Safety department and all production supervisors.
5. Safety department.
6. Production supervisors.
7. Top management.
8. Safety department and production departments.
9. Production departments and safety department.
10. Production departments.
11. Top management and all other management persons.
12. Production departments and safety department.

The leader pointed out that more than half of the items could be made effective by persons represented in the group, and obtained their promise to take action at once. Top management was to be informed of items for them to consider. Reports of this conference were to be delivered personally by the leader, with added oral explanations. Additional written reports were to be distributed to all persons concerned.

By ______________________

Conference Leader

MANAGEMENT CONFERENCE SERIES
CONFERENCE REPORT

Dec. 6, 1946

Problem: What can we do to improve our production scheduling?

Objectives:

1. To understand what production scheduling is.
2. To identify the adverse effects of not having a good scheduling system.
3. To determine wherein our present system is lacking.
4. To determine what we can do to improve our system.

Definition: "Production scheduling" is arranging the sequence of work from receipt of order to shipping of product and properly advising all concerned to anticipate their requirements so as to permit an orderly flow of work and most economical operation of each department.

Opening Statement: The need for reviewing this subject with this group at this time is brought to my attention by the complaints of foremen at different times that they were not aware that certain cores, molds or metal, etc., depending on the department, were required at that particular time. This may be due to enforced schedule changes outside of the control of the production department; for instance, due to breakdown of certain machinery or lack of man power owing to absenteeism or sudden sales pressure for certain castings. Nevertheless, it indicates that probably some tightening up of control needs to be done or at least investigated to see that proper and timely instructions are passed along as soon as possible to all concerned.

The simplest type of production scheduling that can be encountered is the production requirement of one man producing one product for one customer. This becomes more complex with the addition of men on numerous machines of different types and capacities, the products being processed through several departments with a large variety of products, each with varying requirements, to a large customer list. This latter statement seems to apply to our shop and might be illustrated by the fact that we frequently run as high as 700 patterns in one month in six different grades of steel, with considerably different specifications and tolerances to meet for as many as 50 customers for quantities from 1 to 24,000 pieces and weights varying from 3 to 10,000 pounds shipping and 18,000 to 20,000 pounds poured.

Added to this are the various sample runs and rejects to be placed back on schedule because of spoilage from various causes in different stages of production, running all the way from foundry misruns to customer rejects after partial machining.

While production scheduling starts with the receipt of order, their advice is necessary on open schedules and favorable delivery dates to the customer before sales can obtain the order.

Actual scheduling should provide timely advice of requirements to pattern storage for old patterns, pattern shop for new patterns; foundry, core room, cleaning and finishing department, and shipping on specially designed cards and forms to suit, depicting thereon all the essential information to the department concerned, including a freehand perspective sketch of the casting. The master control board is located in the product engineering office and shows by different colored cards the percentage of capacity booked up for each molding floor for a period of 8 months ahead, providing a visible record at all times, being revised and kept up to date as far in advance as possible. The molding and core departments have specially designed display control boards, conveniently located. These are kept up to date 1 week in advance.

In addition to forwarding the proper card to the cleaning and finishing department for each pattern immediately after pouring, the production department furnishes a weekly summary showing the status of all the current patterns in the department with a separate listing of all the castings behind schedule, so that an expediter may be assigned to follow up and obtain quicker action.

The foregoing illustrates the tremendous amount of detail work involved to install and maintain a good schedule system, and efforts, time, and money wasted if not properly followed through.

The matter of issuance of proper and timely instructions has been brought out by other conference leaders as an aid to building morale, to maintaining economic upkeep of machines, and to keeping spoiled work to a minimum; here again, this is stressed on work scheduling showing the necessity of getting this point home.*

Discussion: The first objective did not need any amplification and was covered in the opening statement.

The second objective was furthered by the leader asking for a list of adverse effects that might be the result of not having a good scheduling system, and the following items were suggested:

1. Failure to meet schedules.
2. Confusion locally and generally. "Locally" in this case means certain floors in a department, and "generally" means between departments.
3. Loss of good materials. As an example, cores which have been supplied to the floor and for which there is no longer any requirement, usually have to be destroyed because of scuffed edges through double and triple handling.
4. Loss of production.
5. Creates friction between departments.

* At this point the leader then showed the group a blueprint of a process chart illustrating the routing of all the various printed forms and work performed in the different departments from receipt of inquiry to customer invoice. Typical cards were passed around showing present system. Typed cleaning and finishing department summary sheets and behind schedules were exhibited.

6. More pattern changes than necessary.

7. Less tonnage from present equipment than is possible.

8. Lack of proper segregation.

9. Increased cost due to frequent short runs on large orders when and where it may be possible to run the order solid.

10. Delays sampling to some extent.

11. Equipment may not be available when job is ready to run.

12. Probable underscheduling of some machine at the expense of others.

13. Tends to schedule one department fully and overschedule other departments. This may be due to lack of appreciation of other departments' problems.

14. Tends to lower quality (probable intermixing of Hylastic and high-carbon steel into molds for which the steel was not intended in order to save the molds and avoid "pigging" the steel).

15. Adversely affects work-method standards.

It was the feeling of the group that this section had been inadequately covered, and the third objective, to determine wherein our present system is lacking, was pursued, the following comments being received.

1. Not flexible.

2. Inadequate floor space for proper pattern review.

3. In over-all knowledge of equipment and job requirements. Some of the comments were that the molding department only is fully scheduled; no attempt is made at scheduling cores and chills, etc., and the scheduling does not extend to the reclamation department or tie in the melting with the molding as fully as it might.

4. Time standards. The thought here expressed was the difficulty of establishing proper time standards on a tremendous number of short runs.

5. Lacking forceful follow-up system. An example was given of changing some light work to heavy work in order to meet the metal requirements in No. 2 foundry. The feeling is that this should be anticipated.

6. Enforcement of schedule as set up. It was recommended that, if the scheduling is right in the first place, it should be lived up to instead of being changed by the floor foreman to suit as occasions arise, but that he should first contact the production scheduling department.

7. Dry sand floor not scheduled. It is felt that this would be an advantage in the core room, as this floor could be scheduled.

8. Failure to schedule long runs solid when orders warrant.

In order to further the fourth objective, to determine what we can do to improve our present system, items 2, 3, and 5 were referred to as the most outstanding.

Conclusion: It was determined by the group that there was so much work yet to be done on this subject that the continuance of it into a second conference would be advisable and it was recommended that possibly at that time we have in two or three of the interested supervisors in order that more facts could be provided, discussed, and studied.

It is recommended that the visitors to the next conference be provided with the minutes of this meeting in order to be properly prepared.

By ____________________

Conference Leader

MANAGEMENT CONFERENCE SERIES
CONFERENCE REPORT

Jan. 9, 1946

Problem: What can we do to improve our production scheduling?

Objectives:

1. To understand what production scheduling is.
2. To identify the adverse effects of not having a good scheduling system.
3. To determine wherein our present system is lacking.
4. To determine what we can do to improve our system.

Definition: "Production scheduling" is arranging the sequence of work from receipt of order to shipping of product and properly advising all concerned to anticipate their requirements so as to permit an orderly flow of work and the most economical operation of each department.

Opening Statement: I want to take this opportunity of extending a welcome to our visitors, and have them take active part in this conference and see how these are conducted firsthand. We, in turn, will appreciate their active support and their help to make this a worth-while conference.

This conference is the second one on this subject and the result of one held Dec. 6, 1945, wherein it was felt by the group in session at that time that it was necessary to call in the supervisors directly connected with this problem to help in formulating more accurate conclusions than we could arrive at, owing in part to a lack of factual information; moreover, it was felt that the proper solution to this would be worth while, and could be aided by the thinking of the persons invited to participate in this second conference.

It is to be very definitely understood by all at the outset that the purpose of this conference is to be helpful only and, if there are any weaknesses in our present system, they might properly be aired to see what corrections or changes can be made to improve the system for the over-all benefit of the shop. The conference is not intended to be critical of any individuals in the performance of their work or methods used.

The need for reviewing this subject in the first instance was brought to my attention by remarks of foremen at various times that they were not aware that certain molds, metal, cores, etc., were required at that particular time. This may be due to enforced schedule changes outside of the control of the production scheduling department. For instance, it may be due to breakdown of certain machinery, lack of man power due to absenteeism, or sudden sales pressure for certain castings.

At the first conference a complete review of the present system was made to acquaint the group with most of the pertinent details and complexity of records necessary due to the number of patterns, machines, and customers involved. Mention was made of the follow-up system and weekly summary provided the cleaning and finishing and shipping departments and it is not felt necessary to repeat at this conference.

The group discussion in the initial conference brought out a list of 15 points or items they believed might be the result of not having a good scheduling system and listed the adverse effects on shop operations. It is worth while to review this list briefly with the visitors to determine if they concur with opinions of the conferees. (The list of items was read and all concurred these were essentially correct as stated and no further discussion on these was necessary.)

The leader then recommended a review of the third objective (to determine wherein our present system is lacking), since it applied specifically to this plant in greater detail. These items listed, 1 to 8 inclusive, had previously been posted on the board for ready reference by the group and are restated as follows:

1. Not flexible.

2. Inadequate floor space for proper pattern review.

3. In over-all knowledge of equipment and job requirements. Some of the comments were that the molding department only is fully scheduled; no attempt is made at scheduling cores and chills, etc., and the scheduling does not extend to the reclamation department or tie in the melting with the molding as fully as it might.

4. Time standards. The thought here expressed was the difficulty of establishing proper time standards on a tremendous number of short runs.

5. Lacking forceful follow-up system. An example was given of changing some light work to heavy work in order to meet the metal requirements in No. 2 foundry. The feeling is that this should be anticipated.

6. Enforcement of schedule as set up. It was recommended that, if the scheduling is right in the first place, it should be lived up to instead of being changed by the floor foreman to suit as occasions arise, but that he should first contact the production scheduling department.

7. Dry sand floor not scheduled. It is felt that this would be an advantage in the core room, as this floor could be scheduled.

8. Failure to schedule long runs solid when orders warrant.

Discussion: In the discussion that followed the question of qualification of item 1, the visitors unanimously *disagreed* with this statement, the consensus being that the system is quite flexible. Acceptance of the conference training group was obtained and the item was crossed off as being in error.

The visitors all agreed that items 2 to 7, inclusive, should stand as listed, with changes to examples or reasons given, as these are not pertinent to specific shortcomings of present production scheduling but rather are present because of the over-all coverage of the system. Scheduling of cores, chills, and melted metal are involved, not all of which is under the control of the present scheduling department.

The visitors were of the opinion that item 8 was incorrect, as this is done as much as possible and is rather believed to be the failure of the foremen to consider the over-all picture instead of just considering the effect on their own department operation. It was recommended and agreed by the conferees to cross this item off the list.

Two items were added to the list by the visitors as follows:

1. Too frequently stock items are made up to prevent cutting heats instead of transferring men to other floors to maintain production.

2. Production of stock items creates extra work in the cleaning and finishing department due to extra handling and should be kept to a minimum.

The group agreed that the items as listed were sufficient, and in view of the time allotted for the conference, the leader asked to proceed with the fourth objective, which seeks to determine what we can do to improve our present system, and the following recommendations were made:

1. That we seek to get closer cooperation between production scheduling department and production foremen. The floor foremen should make more use of the master and floor schedule boards. All agreed that much improvement could be made as none of us seem to fully appreciate the other fellow's problems.

2. Increase area for pattern review. All agreed that additional floor space for this purpose is necessary.

3. All agreed that analysis of the delay report should be made daily by the scheduling department and by the foremen; also, it is advisable to discuss it in the planning committee meetings.

4. That generally we are not cognizant of the cumulative effect of minor or small delays and recommend these be recognized and taken into account.

5. That study be made of the possible elimination of old machines and consolidation of work on other floors.

6. That study be given to the scheduling of chills and intricate core rods, dimensional sketches to be provided of the latter.

7. That a follow-up meeting of this group be held week of Mar. 4.

8. That a conference of shop supervisors directly affected in production scheduling be held week of Jan. 14.

9. That all foremen concerned in item 8 be supplied with minutes of this meeting for prior study, and specific cases be considered for correction.

Conclusion: It is the recommendation of this group that this report be submitted to management for consideration and approval of the items as listed, with appointment of a committee to see that the decisions rendered are carried out, reporting back to this group what action has or will be taken.

The timeliness of this subject is recognized, as well as the necessity of immediate action on several items, which the conferees themselves can and will do, being more conscious of the problem confronting both production department and scheduling department as a result of this conference.

By ______________________

Conference Leader

MANAGEMENT CONFERENCE SERIES
CONFERENCE REPORT

May 20, 1947*

Problem: How can each of us do a better job of self-management?

Objectives:

1. To convince ourselves that we can do a better job than we are now doing.

2. To list some important factors that affect our success in our jobs.

3. To list the steps we can take to manage ourselves more effectively.

Definition: "Self-management" means using our individual resources to best advantage. It means accomplishing more on our present jobs, for the ultimate good of society as a whole and for ourselves as individuals.

Self-management involves self-analysis and self-discipline, choosing our actions from the long-range point of view of greatest personal service and success, rather than of present temporary ease or convenience.

Opening Statement: Effective self-management is a constant problem of your leader, and it probably is a problem of each man in this group. No person performs up to 100 per cent of his or her potential capacity. That is the result of being human and heir to all human weakness. There is a wide range of performance when comparing the effective-

* This is the report of a guided conference. Almost every question asked by the leader was a direct question to a named individual. This conference required prepared questions asked in prepared sequence. Answers provoked informal discussion. Every point recorded in the report was planned by the leader. Many, if not most, of them would have been offered in an unguided conference, but not in desired sequence and not always adequately expressed. It was an overtime conference, requiring 2 full hours of discussion. The group was interested and cooperative and this conference was talked about for weeks afterward.

ness of different people. Some persons may consistently perform reasonably near their maximum capacity. Others use no more than 10 to 20 per cent of their potential or maximum capacity. Because even the most effective persons can improve to some degree and because most of us are so far from our potential, it can be accurately stated that all of us can have whatever we desire in life within surprisingly high limits, if we are *willing to pay the price*. Most of us would say that we are willing to pay the price, but analysis of our actions reveal surrender to desire for pleasure, to desire for rest or relief from effort, or to difficulties of many kinds.

Success is not always measured in terms of popularity or high office. It is measured in terms of service to society and in terms of personal satisfaction. The measure of success is not always material wealth or attainment of high rank. It is, rather, the distance traveled from one's starting place to where he finishes his lifework, and the number and seriousness of the difficulties overcome along the way.

Discussion: The discussion of the conference group was first directed to a consideration of the definition of "self-management." The leader pointed out that the phraseology was his own, but that he hoped the meaning and significance of the wording as recorded would meet with the approval of the members of the group. It was recognized that with the same mental picture in mind, individuals of the group most certainly would have used different phraseology. The leader's suggestion was accepted and the inherent thoughts of the definition were accepted.

There was some discussion with respect to the relationship of service and individual success, and there was discussion of the part that the present job plays in a life program. The leader discovered that there was no disagreement with the thought expressed in objective 1, that is, that all of us can do a better job than we are now doing. For that reason, no more time was spent on objective 1, and the discussion progressed immediately to objective 2.

At this point the leader, working with the group, built a list of factors that affect our success in our present jobs. The list follows:

1. *Natural aptitude.* Natural aptitude refers to a liking for, or a natural ability for, certain kinds of work or activity. Some children early show signs of musical aptitude or ability. Others show signs of mathematical ability. It was agreed that, among other factors, natural aptitude does have a bearing upon our success in our present job. If through some mistake or through lack of planning we find ourselves trying to do work for which we have no natural aptitude or ability, we will very surely make less progress than if we did possess such natural aptitude.

2. *The amount of education and training an individual receives.*

   a. In school. It was pointed out that this refers to formal education before going on a job. This school education can be meager, or it can be long extended and very complete.

   b. On-the-job training. This does not refer to formal school education, but, as the phrase implies, it is the training of how to do the details of an assigned job for wages. It involves the know-how, sometimes manual, sometimes mental. It often involves judgment and the knowledge of miscellaneous facts.

   c. Training in the home. This involves habits built up by one's parents, whether or not the youth is trained in doing a job properly, whether certain habits are formed that strengthen one's character, whether there is development of judgment in the growing child, and all of those habits that have to do with success in later life.

   d. Self-education. This refers to programs of self-improvement adopted by the individual after employment and taken, for the most part, on his or her personal time. This will be referred to in greater detail at another place in this report.

3. *The quality and quantity of counsel and supervision one receives from his or her supervisor.* The greater emphasis should be on the quality of this counsel and supervision. No subordinate should be expected to do his work day after day without counsel and supervision. The average person needs to know how well or how poorly he is doing his tasks, and he needs to be constructively advised how to improve. The supervision should not be confined to faultfinding and criticism, but rather it should always be given from the standpoint of developing and improving the individual.

4. *Our own character.* Involved in this are integrity, honesty, morals, ethics, humility, and the willingness to work at mediocre jobs, even though they are disagreeable.

5. *The amount of effort the individual puts forth.* This requires little explanation. Some people do as little as they can and some do as much as they can, and there is a very wide range in between.

6. *Initiative and resourcefulness.* Initiative means that we have a self-starter in our make-up. We do not need to be goaded or prodded to perform our tasks. Resourcefulness means that when difficulties present themselves, we invent ways of overcoming the difficulties. If one trial fails, we make another attempt.

7. *A realization of the need for self-management.* It is true that some people do not realize that effectiveness in our daily tasks and in making a success for ourselves requires self-management. They are not aware of the fact that so many things we do can be eliminated altogether, or they can be timed better, or the work itself can be shortened by improvements; or they do not realize that their sense of values should be developed so that they can choose intelligently between this or that desirable thing and choose the one that will be most lastingly helpful.

8. *Perseverance.* Not only do we need good honest effort, as pointed out in item 5, but we need consistent, sustained, persevering effort.

9. *The existence of a plan for the job.* Many people work from hour to hour doing the thing that seems most obvious or doing that which accidently attracts their attention. Many times it is necessary to search for those things which are not obvious or to plan for emergencies rather than to trust to luck that the thing we choose to do at the moment is the timely and proper thing to do. In this connection, there ought to be a plan for one's future. The present job may be only a stepping stone in a life plan. Too few of us have a life plan. We fail to look beyond the present job. It is the sign of an intelligent and farseeing individual to look beyond the present job, sometimes years, and set a goal for which the present job is only one of several stepping stones.

10. *The capacity for analysis of oneself and of daily problems.* It is necessary for one to find out one's weaknesses and one's strong points. The weaknesses need to be eliminated or strengthened, whichever is required. Job problems need to be analyzed to speed their solution or prevent their recurrence.

11. *Ambition.* Ambition means the desire to accomplish something, to achieve a desired end. This means that we have a goal to work for instead of existing from day to day, being satisfed with whatever pleasures the present day brings, with no effort to plan for bigger and better pleasures tomorrow, or for the indefinite future.

At this point it became clear that a number of significant factors affecting a person's success on the present job had been listed. If only a part of the list were recognized and used, without doubt any person could make significant improvement in his everyday performance. However, in keeping with objective 3, the thinking of the group took concrete form and they listed steps that the individual can take for the purpose of more successful self-management.

1. *Every individual should organize a plan for his present job.* He should try out the plan and, in the light of experience with the plan, reorganize it and note the results. The reorganizing, *i.e.*, the improvement, should continue until there is a satisfactory plan worked out, which should last until new factors enter the picture.

This organizing of one's job or planning how to do one's job refers of course to assignments where the method of doing is left to the judgment or discretion of the doer. It does not refer to routine factory or office jobs.

A point was made that in industrial organizations the organizing of one's job very frequently requires a study of how one's job fits into the organization as a whole. Without this understanding of how his job affects other jobs, and how other jobs affect his job, few persons can do thorough planning for their own jobs.

2. *To set up a personal improvement program.*

   a. One of the things all of us can do is to read selected articles or texts. This can be on items directly concerned with one's everyday job. It could be trade magazines; it could be textbooks; it could be the experiences of other persons in similar capacities.

   b. Enrollment in correspondence courses. Sometimes local classes are not available. In such case correspondence courses are helpful and are effective in full measure corresponding to the sincerity and effort of the person taking the course.

   c. Attendance of lectures, forums, etc.

   d. Enrollment in local extension courses. Many times there are available locally courses that deal with the content of one's everyday work. It is often worth while to enroll in these courses, if for no other reason than to keep up to date and to keep freshly informed regarding details that might slip one's mind but which may be needed at any time.

e. On-the-job classes, or individual contacts. This refers to short intensive courses within the organization itself, or, if not classes, it refers to chosen contacts with persons who have experience and who can give advice and information that will be helpful.

f. A physical-fitness program. For long-range as well as for present success, every one of us should safeguard his health. We need a certain amount of play, and we need to be intelligent in the food we eat and in the hours that we keep.

3. *Each individual should make a thorough analysis of himself, or have it done by a competent person.* This analysis should be studied seriously and the truth accepted. The analysis is necessary to discover traits which may be offensive to others or which betray weaknesses in planning or in execution of one's duties.

4. *After an appropriate interval of time, measure the progress that has been attained.* Without some measurement of progress or attention to that detail, one may fail to make any progress at all; one may even slip backward. This periodic checking up is essential to forward progress.

5. *Choose competent persons to give counsel.* Most of us are acquainted with persons for whom we have respect, persons who also have tact and diplomacy and integrity, and if we can prevail upon such persons to counsel us and if we will be strong enough to profit by such counsel, we can truly progress and improve ourselves.

6. *We should seek until we find some one person whom we want as an individual counselor,* apart from the ones mentioned in the preceding item, a counselor who will not wait for our own approach to him but who will accept the responsibility of keeping a sort of watch over us, and, when

it is necessary, prompt us to do what we need to do or help us to do it.

Conclusion: Each member of the group was asked whether or not this series of six steps contained one or more which he was not doing or which he was doing in insufficient amount. If so, would he accept the responsibility of taking action and reporting on that action before the close of this training program? Each member agreed that there was one or more steps that he should take and he did agree to begin work and to report progress before the end of the current training program. The leader pointed out that only by acceptance of responsibility and by some form of follow-up could action be ensured to follow the discussion.

In conclusion, both the leader and the members of the group are looking forward eagerly to the time when the report of progress will be made.

By ____________________.
Conference Leader

SUPERINTENDENTS' CONFERENCE SERIES
CONFERENCE REPORT

Mar. 25, 1947

Problem: How can we get workers to understand the economic cost of absenteeism?

Objectives:

1. To list reasons, true or false, for absenteeism.

2. To list methods to bring home to workers the cost of absenteeism.

3. To determine which of the items in objective 2 are practical and which we shall apply now.

Definitions: By "economic cost" is meant (1) cost to the worker, (2) cost to the company, and (3) cost to the consumers.

Opening Statement: We all realize the serious problem confronting us today as a result of absenteeism. This problem of absenteeism reached serious proportions during the recent war and it was felt that possibly at the cessation of hostilities the problem of absenteeism would be greatly reduced. However, this has not been the case.

This absenteeism seriously affects the morale of all the workers in the plant, as well as the pocketbooks of every individual. It has sometimes been said that the only one affected through absenteeism is the absentee himself. This is not true, as it has been definitely shown that absenteeism has a direct bearing on the costs of products being manufactured, and the costs of these products are reflected in the purchases the worker must make.

There are a great many methods of attacking the problem of absenteeism. In my opinion the best method to reduce absenteeism is by education and trying to make the employees realize that they are suffering a severe economic loss when we have an excessive absenteeism rate.

Various methods have been tried at penalizing, etc., and

none have been too successful. Therefore, for our problem today I have chosen "How can we get the worker to understand the economic cost of absenteeism?" We will therefore proceed with our discussion and list the items under objective 1.

Discussion: Discussion brought out the following list of true and false reasons for absence from work:

1. Sickness, individual or family
2. Death in family
3. Payday sickness
4. Personal reasons
5. Just want a day off (with no apparent reason)
6. Car broke down (transportation)
7. Overslept
8. Weather, bad or good
9. Don't like boss or job
10. Job too tough or complicated
11. Fatigue
12. Shopping for another job
13. Outside work

The leader asked for practical ideas that could be put to work to reduce absenteeism. The following list was suggested:

1. Keep records of absenteeism and post in department, showing loss of wages.

2. Keep record of individual absence, including loss of wages, and discuss with individual privately.

3. Penalties.

4. Post on bulletin boards the plant-wide cost of absenteeism.

5. Furnish foremen more plant-wide information on absenteeism, including cost.

6. Do not fill absentee turns with premium time (which may result in loss of time to rest of crew).

7. Furnish supervisors a short course in economics, in

terms of our operation and production, for use in talks to the workers.

8. Show what can be bought with lost wages of workers, this to be in general terms. No specific cases.

9. Mail work schedule to home.

10. Foremen hold meetings with their men to discuss absenteeism. This to be done only where absenteeism rate is excessive, and such meetings must be conducted diplomatically.

11. Man's loss of earnings due to his absenteeism to be shown (*a*) on pay stub or (*b*) slip with check.

12. A large bulletin board to show by departments the number of absentees daily. Also more general publicity on absenteeism.

13. Secure union cooperation.

With respect to steps to be taken now, it was agreed by the conferees that only those items be recommended which have unanimous approval of the conference. It was felt that this unanimous approval will lend more weight to the objective 3 recommendations, and what does come out will be sound and practical. The unanimously approved items are as follows:

1. Supervisors be furnished a short course in economics in terms of our operation and production, and that the foremen hold meetings with their men on the subject of absenteeism and use such information furnished to make the meeting interesting and constructive. It was felt that this short course in economics would have a real value for our supervisors in many ways other than just on the problem of absenteeism.

2. A record be kept of individual absence, including loss of wages, and that this record be discussed with the absentee privately, pointing out what his absenteeism is costing him and his fellow employees. Also that general publicity be put out, showing what can be purchased with the lost wages of the absentee workers.

3. It was the unanimous opinion of the conferees that

last-resort and final action in correcting absenteeism should be a consistent, plant-wide penalty for the absentee. However, it was recognized that a great deal of thought will have to be given to the problem, as to when this penalty be applied.

Conclusion: Some of the recommended action can and will be taken by persons in this conference group. Other action requires the approval and/or action of top management, and in such case the conference leader with one or more members of this group will present these recommendations to top management and will seek their approval and/or action.

By ______________________

Conference Leader

SUPERINTENDENTS' CONFERENCE SERIES
CONFERENCE REPORT

Dec. 3, 1946

Problem: To determine what we can do to conserve maintenance, repair, and supply materials.

Objectives:

1. To list some of the materials concerned in our problem.

2. To list some causes for waste or loss as related to these materials.

3. To determine what we can do to conserve some of these materials.

Opening Statement: Each one of us uses, or is responsible for the use of, materials of one kind or another for maintenance or repair purposes or in the form of supplies.

Labor unrest and the unsettled postwar conditions make this probably the most difficult period we have faced as to our ability to obtain adequate supplies.

We spend more than 6 million dollars per year for maintenance, repair, and supply materials, and if we could conserve 10 per cent of this item we would in effect be releasing materials to a value of $600,000 and thus would be helping ourselves to solve our problem of supply. Not only would we save money, we would eliminate certain problems of supply and certain internal operating problems. It is worth our while to turn our attention to this problem. A small percentage of 6 million dollars is a very large sum of money, which could be used advantageously some other way.

Discussion:

Objective 1: The following materials were suggested by the conferees:

Lumber—construction, blocking, pattern
Rubber products—hose, tires, belting
Brick
Electrical materials

Hardware
Bearing metals
Antifriction bearings
Lubricants
Hand tools
Castings—bronze, iron, steel

Objective 2: The following causes of loss or waste were suggested:

Improper storage of item needing protection from weather, moisture, dirt, theft, etc.

Carelessness in handling, resulting in damages or misplacement

Overdrawing from stores and failing to return excess materials

Improper application

Theft

Poor inspection of material when received resulting in failure to note poor quality or damaged materials

Overlubrication

Lack of information as to value, suitable substitutes

Duplication—where two or more departments use same materials but have no system of interchange

Objective 3: There was a serious and healthy discussion as to what might be done to conserve materials, resulting in the following suggestions:

1. Better control of requisitions on stores and purchasing departments by supervision.
2. Confine quantities requisitioned to requirements.
3. Develop a knowledge of such requirements by studying job to be done.
4. Educate those responsible for using materials through the means of foremen's meetings or personal contact, informative bulletins issued by the stores department, articles of general information in the plant publication.
5. See that deliveries are prompt and frequent to avoid necessity of keeping too much on hand in departments.

6. Supervision by issuing department to prevent overdrawing and misapplication and to suggest use of proper substitutes.

7. Better control over materials duplicated by various departments by stocking these items in stores department.

8. A central control record of all materials to avoid duplication and take more advantage of quantity prices.

9. Reduce theft by a better system of gate passes.

Conclusion: It was agreed by the conferees that we carry out the first three and part of the fourth items of the above list; that items 5 and 6 and that the part of item 4 pertaining to bulletins be the responsibility of the stores department; that items 7 and 8 be submitted to the management for approval and action; and that item 9 be recommended to management for further study. It was also agreed that further conferences on materials would be beneficial.

By ________________________

Conference Leader

SUPERINTENDENTS' CONFERENCE SERIES
CONFERENCE REPORT

Oct. 31, 1947

Problem: How to obtain a better relationship between the various levels of supervision.

Objectives:

1. To understand what the supervisor and his subordinates owe one another.

2. To understand how to work harmoniously with one another.

3. To outline what is needed in order to do a better job in human relationships between supervisors and subordinates.

Opening Statement: In most organizations the relationships between supervisors and subordinates at any level are a result of accidental growth rather than any specific planning. It is much the same as Topsy in "Uncle Tom's Cabin," who just grew. In most cases supervisors have not given intensive thought to their responsibilities towards their subordinates, and in more cases subordinates have not thought deeply or given sufficient consideration to what they owe their supervisors of the organization as a whole.

Much of the discord, discontent, and confusion that exists in many industries today is not a sign of a lack of intelligence, or a lack of honesty, or lack of character, but it is solely due to failure to give thought to relationships that involve the fundamentals of human conduct of one person with another. It is the opinion of thinking persons that a discussion of these fundamentals would work toward a better understanding of supervisor and subordinates, regardless of what level. It is true of a foreman and his assistant foreman. It is true of a factory manager and his immediate staff. It is hoped that, as a result of this discussion, the members of this discussion group will understand these fundamentals and will be prepared to put various aspects of these fundamentals into practice.

Discussion: The leader asked as his first discussion question, "What does a supervisor look for when he is selecting a subordinate; that is, what qualities or qualifications does he look for?" The following list was offered:

1. Honesty and sincerity.
2. Knowledge of the job.

   Comment: This does not necessarily mean familiarity with present job details, but it does mean the basic training required for the particular kind of work to be done.

3. Ability to get along with others.
4. Aggressiveness and initiative.
5. Loyalty.

   Comment: There was some discussion regarding loyalty and there were brought out a number of ways in which loyalty or disloyalty could be manifested.

6. Dependability.
7. Pleasing personality.
8. Good health.
9. Good character.

   Comment: The pros and cons of this requirement were debated with no attempt to arrive at a conclusive answer to apply in all cases. It seemed to be the opinion of the majority that a good character would be not only desirable but an asset in almost all cases. It was pointed out that in some cases a person of questionable character is known to be doing a good job in the plant.

10. Willingness to work.

    Comment: By this is meant the willingness to do a good day's work without shirking or stalling or just attempting to get by.

11. Willingness to follow instructions.
12. Willingness to accept responsibility.

Comment: The question was asked as to the relative importance of this item. It was the practically unanimous opinion that willingness to accept responsibility rates near the top of this list.

13. Ambition.

Comment: This list could be amplified indefinitely but enough items have been recorded to accomplish the objectives desired.

The next question asked by the leader was, "What does the supervisor owe his subordinates?"

Comment: Attention was called to the fact that as the supervisor looks for such an imposing list of qualifications, he expects certain standards of performance and certain attitudes on the part of his subordinates. What does he do to help them? What does he owe them?

The following list was given in answer to the question:

1. Cooperation.
2. An adequate training and adjustment period.
3. Frankness.
4. Counsel or good advice.

Comment: In connection with items 3 and 4 it was emphasized that the supervisor owes his subordinate constructive criticism instead of mere faultfinding. He owes him good advice, which may be a specific application or it may be merely general.

5. Credit for good work.
6. The supervisor should prepare and furnish all needed information promptly.

Comment: Withholding this information may seriously handicap the subordinate in the discharge of his assignment.

7. The supervisor owes his subordinate common everyday courtesy.

8. The supervisor owes his subordinate an outline of his assignments, duties, and responsibilities. This includes limits of his authority and responsibility.

9. The supervisor owes his subordinate his confidence.

10. He owes him tolerance and patience.

11. He owes him backing and support.

> *Comment:* Even if the subordinate is in error in his decision, the supervisor owes him explanations and counsel; and in some cases, even support in a sincere though mistaken decision.

12. The supervisor owes his subordinates fair financial remunerations insofar as he is in possession of authority to do so.

13. The supervisor owes his subordinates opportunity to achieve promotion.

> *Comment:* In this connection the supervisor should be willing to release his subordinate in favor of a better job. To prevent such opportunity for a better job immediately causes loss of interest, loss of effectiveness, and sooner or later loss of morale and loss of loyalty.

14. The supervisor owes his subordinate loyalty in the same ways that the subordinate owes loyalty.

> *Comment:* There was one discussion as to the number of ways in which the supervisor can show loyalty or the lack of it.

15. The supervisor owes it to his subordinates to be receptive to their sincere suggestions for improvements.

The next question asked by the leader was, "What does the subordinate owe his supervisor?" The following list was developed:

1. His best efforts.
2. Loyalty.

3. Cooperation.
4. Respect.
5. Frankness and the courage of his own convictions.

Comment: Failure to express his sincere opinion is in a very definite way "short changing" the supervisor because it deprives the supervisor of needed points of view. Also, since the subordinate may be closer to the problem, he should pass on to his supervisor certain items of information which he alone will possess and which the supervisor needs in his administration.

6. Willingness to take instruction and to obey orders.

7. Willingness and ability to pass on instruction and information properly to other persons concerned; for example, to his own subordinates.

8. Pride in his job, in his department, and in his company.

9. The subordinate owes it not only to himself but to his supervisor to make honest efforts at self-improvement.

10. The subordinate owes his supervisor a continually improved performance.

The final question asked by the leader was "Considering the lists that have been developed in the preceding hour, in what ways can we, as supervisors and subordinates, improve our relationships with one another?"

1. We can do a better job in passing on information than we have done before. This may include not delaying and possibly it may include being more accurate in information that is passed on. It may also in some cases include giving information that is not now given.

2. In some cases, perhaps the supervisors can do more of personal counseling than heretofore. It should be pointed out that these are informational person-to-person talks, where the subordinate has opportunity to express his points of view, to ask and receive guidance, and are not limited

to an opportunity for the supervisor to give needed criticism or advice.

These "twosomes" should be held regularly, not necessarily daily or weekly, but possibly monthly, and are not to be confused with the daily brief salutations of supervisor and subordinate, where there is a casual greeting and perhaps a little discussion of current events. It should be pointed out that this particular item could have been discussed longer had there been sufficient time.

3. There was mention but there was no time to adequately discuss the value of organization charts and job descriptions. It appears that these devices are used in this plant with considerable success.

Conclusion: Finally, the leader pointed out that this was not only a demonstration conference, but should be considered as a work conference where action should follow the discussion and where every person, if possible, should find something said in this discussion that he could use to his own advantage, either as a supervisor or as a subordinate. Without such action, the time spent in this discussion has been wasted.

There was general agreement that this discussion had clarified certain concepts and had strengthened resolves of certain individuals to do a better job than heretofore.

By ______________________
Conference Leader

FOREMEN'S CONFERENCE SERIES
CONFERENCE REPORT

Nov. 1, 1945

Problem: How can we develop morale in our plant?

Objectives:

1. To understand the meaning of the word "morale."
2. To determine what factors tend to weaken morale.
3. To identify those things which promote better morale.
4. To determine what we need to do in our organization to build and maintain high morale.

Definition: Morale is a state of mind. To develop morale is to build the worker into such a mental state as to instill zeal, spirit, hope, and confidence in his fellow worker, in his foreman, and in his job.

Opening Statement: One of the most difficult types of labor unrest to deal with is the "slowdown," and we can truthfully say that we are well acquainted with such a condition. Here, in our plant, production has fallen off to an alarmingly low figure. The efficiency of this plant may be only slightly higher than 50 per cent. These conditions have been growing with the years. In comparing our present production with that of 2 years ago, we now produce only five heats a day from our electric furnace, whereas we were getting eight to nine heats a day 2 years ago. All this low production is done in spite of better equipment, work simplification, and less fatigue. It seems that workers are working to a prearranged schedule: that is to say, the cleaning and finishing departments will not clean any more tonnage than the foundry will produce, and the foundry will not produce any more than the cleaning and finishing department will clean.

The other day I had occasion to talk with one of our salesmen. He was very much alarmed about our production. He cited where 300 castings were promised for shipment in the past month, and the customer received only 29 castings. At that rate, we know, we will not retain that customer much longer. What has brought that condition upon us? I would say, it is a direct result of bad morale.

What is morale? Simply defined, "morale" is a state of mind. When a worker, of his own accord or through organized false propaganda, gets it into his head that the company is not giving him a square deal, when he does not like the foreman, or when he wishes to protest some company regulations, then we should expect morale to be low.

There is only one practical way to eliminate "slowdowns," *i.e.,* to head them off before they happen. To do that calls for a program that has for its aim the building up and maintaining of the highest possible degree of worker morale. A worker whose heart and soul is in his job will not listen to obstructionists who ask him to "lay down." If he has confidence in the company that he represents, he is unlikely to stand for slackers in his department. While there are always a few radicals in every plant who make a good deal of noise, if the morale of the majority of workers is good, this radical group will have very little real influence upon the actions of the workers.

Building a high morale costs money, but it pays handsome dividends!

Discussion: The definition of the word "morale" was discussed by the group. This discussion led to the accomplishment of the first objective. The definition as given by the leader was not altered in the discussion.

The second objective was furthered when the leader asked for a list of those things that tend to weaken the worker's morale. The following factors were offered by the group:

1. Organized outside pressure.
2. Poor working conditions.

    a. Poor ventilation.
    b. Poor lighting.
    c. Inadequate heating facilities.

d. Poor arrangement of the working area.
e. Poor housekeeping.

3. Lack of a sound incentive plan. It was pointed out that a wage incentive plan is not a cure for all evils. A liking for his fellow workers, good working conditions, confidence in his foreman, and a certain degree of loyalty to his company are some of the things that have a marked effect on the worker's morale.
4. Wage inequalities.
5. Suspicion.

a. Trickery on part of foreman.
b. Teachings by outside organized forces.

6. Workers placed in wrong occupation.
7. Evidence of indecision on the part of management to foreman, and foreman to worker. Some of the causes of this indecision are

a. Lack of information.
b. Poor planning.
c. Overlapping authority.

8. Showing favoritism.
9. Fear of temporary layoff. It was pointed out that in this plant production has dropped off after a certain layoff due to the fear that a backlog will again be built up in another department.
10. Failure of the foreman to recognize the worker's qualities and abilities.
11. Failure of the seniority system to recognize ability.
12. The foreman is impatient with the workers.

The next question presented by the leader was, "What are those things which promote and build morale?" The group offered the following list:

1. Better instruction, by means of a good indoctrination system. By the means of a good indoctrination system the worker would be informed of the many advantages offered

by our company, such as insurance policies, hospitalization plans, employees benefit associations, wages comparable to other like industries, safety rules, medical care, good working conditions, etc.

2. Understanding by the foreman of attitudes and points of view of his workers.

3. Good approach—more is to be gained by asking the worker to do a job rather than demanding that he do it.

4. Knowing how to correct the worker properly.

5. Give credit where credit is due.

6. Give the worker a clear understanding of the departmental problems.

7. Institute a foremen's training program through conference leadership training to solve many of our foreman-worker problems.

8. Good working conditions.

9. Good housekeeping—a clean shop is very important in building workers' morale.

10. Making the worker feel that he is part of the company.

11. Good-wage incentives and other incentives.

12. Good foreman personality.

13. Good communication system. All information from management should come to the workers through regular-line organization channels. This would eliminate the grapevine system of getting information to the workers first. If management does not reach the foreman first, the foreman loses confidence in the management, and the worker in turn loses confidence in the foreman.

In approaching the fourth objective, the leader asked this question: "What do we need to do in our organization to build and maintain a high morale?" It was recommended by the group that management plan a series of foreman's conferences on human-relation problems. The ultimate goal of these conferences is to establish a better understanding between workers and management and eventually to bring about an increase in production.

In addition, every member of the group accepted the responsibility of taking stock of his own performance with respect to relations with his workers, and indeed with all others in the plant. And after having taken stock or made a self-analysis, and having recognized wherein he needed to improve, each man agreed to attempt to make such improvement. This should result in each person's becoming better informed as to how workers think, and why, and how to gain their confidence and supply them with facts and sound points of view.

Still further, attention to the workers' comfort, convenience, and material interest can be given within present authority. And if all these things are sincerely done, improvement of worker morale is sure to follow.

Conclusion: A brief review of the foregoing discussion was made, and the group reaffirmed their thinking and their pledge to action.

By ____________________
Conference Leader

FOREMEN'S CONFERENCE SERIES
CONFERENCE REPORT

Nov. 1, 1945

Problem: What factors should be included in a fair promotional, demotional, and layoff system?

Objectives:

1. To identify the present plan of promotion, demotion, and layoff.

2. To determine how the present plan hinders production.

3. To identify those things which promote a more effective plan.

4. To suggest a system that would be fair to the employees and help to increase and maintain full production.

Definition: The present system of promotion, demotion, and layoff of employees is based on two governing factors: length of service, and ability to perform the work skillfully and efficiently with the emphasis (in practice) on length of service.

Opening Statement: Under the seniority ruling, in some instances an unqualified employee has been promoted and the higher skilled men on the job have been laid off.

Some labor organizations have used seniority to its highest extent when inducing employees to join the organization. Some employees become lazy and, knowing that they have more seniority than the fellows back of them, take the attitude of "You can't lay me off." In this state of laziness, schedules are not met according to the customers' requirements; therefore, customers cancel their orders, production goes downgrade, and, when there aren't any production orders, men have to be demoted and laid off. Absenteeism falls in the same category. As an example, on Friday, Nov. 23, the day following Thanksgiving, there were approximately 45 employees absent throughout the entire plant.

Several years ago on a particular unit machine, a crew often made 450 flasks in an 8-hour shift. At the present time, working under conditions as stated in the above paragraphs and even though laborsaving machines have been installed and the base rates increased, the production rate had dropped to 180 flasks per shift, which is 270 flasks under what the machine and employees are capable of turning out.

Discussion: The leader asked the group to analyze the definition as it appeared on the board, and after a short discussion a few minor changes were made and the definition was accepted by the group.

The second objective was approached by the leader asking the group to prepare a list of those things which point out how our present plan hinders production. The following list was offered:

1. Decreases production.
2. Causes improper placement of men on the job.
3. Causes poor quality of work.
4. Causes dissension among employees.
5. Results in loss of customers—schedules not met, customers cancel and do not reorder.
6. Tends to develop improper attitude toward jobs.
7. Leads to loss of good workers—unqualified men are promoted and skilled men demoted or laid off.
8. Lowers supervisors' morale and decreases their effectiveness.

The leader then proceeded to ask the group to suggest a list of those things which would help or assist in promoting a more effective plan. The following list was submitted:

1. *Union should recognize ability.* The group felt that when considering the ability of a worker we should consider the performance of the worker from the standpoint of quality and quantity of work produced. This would require selling the idea to the union officials.

2. *Install a merit system.* The group felt that any merit system chosen should enable us to prove the ability of the

employee and should be based on performance records. Ability should be recognized in wage payment, in promotions, and in retention on the pay roll in times of personnel reduction.

3. *Establish a reasonable learning time for proving ability on a particular job classification.* There was some discussion at this point, and one member of the group pointed out examples where learning periods were too long. The union representatives would say, "Give him a try for another week or so." Then when the 45-day period was about up and the worker still showed no ability to perform the job, the foreman would suggest the worker be removed from that job. The union representative then would say, "You better keep him because if you didn't plan to retain him you should have taken him off the job earlier in his probationary period."

It was the consensus of the group that the learning period should be a limited number of days, and the worker at the end of his period should be removed or retained in his new position.

In the discussion of the fourth objective, it was decided that no new points could be added to those listed under objective 3.

Conclusion: The conference group agreed that this discussion crystallized the thinking of all the conferees and enlarged their viewpoint. The group through this report requests top management to consider seriously the recommendations of this conference, especially with respect to a so-called "merit rating plan" and to a well-considered and reasonable learning period.

By ____________________
Conference Leader

FOREMEN'S CONFERENCE SERIES
CONFERENCE REPORT

July 31, 1946

Problem: To analyze a case problem in human relations.

Objectives:

1. To list the mistakes made by the various characters involved.

2. To formulate some rules to be observed for the purpose of preventing problems such as the one discussed in this conference.

List of Characters:

Plant superintendent	Henry Morton
Foreman of heat-treating department	Harry Prentiss
A workman in the heat-treating department	Bill Smith

Opening Statement: For the past 10 years your conference leader has been asking senior executives, managers of industrial relations departments, and personnel managers what was the most important single qualification for an executive. Invariably, the answer has been skill in human relations or, in other words, leadership ability. Leadership ability is effected by the training received by the child when very young, when it is still unable to walk. The kind of training that the parents give through the growing years will determine that child's response to other persons and the child's ability to get along agreeably and harmoniously with others. Teachers in the schools, from the primary grades on through high school and university, also exert influence. The experience of an individual on his first job also has an influence. In other words, skill in human relations, or leadership, takes years to develop. It is very improbable that a mature individual, forty-one years of age or older, and especially older, will change quickly in his relations with other people. If improvement is to be made, it will be made very slowly.

On the contrary, job know-how can be supplied in a few years at most, and a sufficient amount can usually be supplied in a few months, sometimes in a few weeks.

These executives whom your conference leader has questioned have stated that if they must choose between a person high in leadership and low in job know-how and another person high in job know-how and low in leadership ability, they would always choose the person high in leadership ability. They would do so knowing that the job know-how could be supplied much more easily than the leadership qualifications that were lacking. The study of a case problem should help us understand the importance of leadership ability.

Harry Prentiss was an engineering graduate with approximately 4 years of industrial experience in a technical capacity. He had never been a foreman. Harry Prentiss was courteous to his workers, but not friendly. He did not attempt to sell himself to them, never asked for advice, but he always gave his orders and instructions courteously and quietly.

Bill Smith, one of the workmen in the heat-treating department, was fifty-five years old, a high-school graduate, and had had between 25 and 30 years of practical heat-treating experience. The heat-treating department employed 11 other men besides Bill Smith.

A difficulty arose in the heat-treating department with respect to a large casting. The processing of this casting included heating it to a very high temperature and then immersing it in a bath of oil, the oil being mechanically agitated. Approximately one-third of the castings developed cracks and were scrapped. The castings were large, and the amount of metal, plus the amount of labor expended, made a very heavy loss on each one scrapped.

Harry, in thinking about the problem, wondered if discontinuing the agitation of the oil when the casting was in the oil bath would help. He spoke to Morton, who said he had no ideas about it, that it was Harry's problem, and Harry should do as he thought best.

Harry went to the heat-treating department, and Bill Smith was ready to put a casting in the oil bath. Harry said, "Don't turn on the agitator this time, Bill." But Bill insisted he should. Harry insisted firmly that it should *not* be turned on. Neither one would yield. A quarrel ensued and hot words passed between foreman and his subordinate. Finally, Harry stepped over toward the switch to shut off the agitator, which Bill had just turned on.

Bill stepped in front of him and barred his way, saying, "Don't touch that switch! I'm in charge of this operation."

Confronted by such a situation, Harry was confused. He knew he was wrong in having engaged in a quarrel and did not know what he should do. He returned to his office to think about it. The afternoon passed, and he had done nothing. At the close of the day he learned three out of eight castings processed that day had cracked.

The following morning, Harry called Bill into his office and told him that for insubordination on the preceding day, he (Bill) was to go home for 2 weeks without pay. Bill was still angry and said he would not take it. He went to Superintendent Morton's office and said he was being sent home because three castings were cracked and he had carefully processed them all as originally instructed. Morton listened to his story and then sent for Harry. In the three-man discussion Morton supported Harry's decision. But it came out that about 10 days preceding this incident Harry had made a remark about Bill to one of Bill's "buddies." Harry was kidding, but the buddy related it to Bill as a very slighting and unfriendly remark.

Harry, backed up by Morton, again ordered Bill to go home for 2 weeks without pay. Bill departed.

On the fourth day following, because of increased need for man power in the heat-treating department, Morton and Harry agreed to send for Bill before his time was up. He came back. He was "cocky," feeling he was a man they could not do without. He refused to take Harry's orders.

So what was to be done?

Discussion: At this point the leader asked for a listing of mistakes made by the three principals in this problem, and the following were listed:

Smith's Mistakes:

1. He carried a grudge.

2. He failed to ask the reason for a change in procedure when such request should have been a natural thing to do.

3. He knowingly and willfully disobeyed orders.

4. He was "set in his ways," *i.e.*, was satisfied with his way of thinking and doing.

5. He displayed a belligerent attitude.

Prentiss's Mistakes:

1. He never tried to gain the confidence of his workers.

2. He failed to give reasons for a change in procedure.

3. He belittled a worker, behind the worker's back, to the worker's "buddies."

4. He failed to ask Bill (a worker of long experience) for suggestions when the casting trouble first appeared.

5. He lost his temper and quarreled with a subordinate.

6. He admitted no error when he next talked to Smith.

7. He handed out a punishment that was hasty and ill considered and probably was too severe, all things being considered.

8. He used too much time in reaching a decision after an emergency in which his authority had been challenged.

9. He later was a willing party in reversing a disciplinary action.

Morton's Mistakes:

1. When he listened to Smith, he by-passed Prentiss.

2. On at least two occasions he acted hastily without having the facts or considering the effect of his action.

a. Approved without investigating Prentiss's idea regarding the cooling of the casting.

b. Concurred in an ill-advised disciplinary action.

3. He shared responsibility for reversing a ruling. (If the ruling had been reversed because in reviewing it there was an opinion it was a mistaken ruling, the reversal would have had a better flavor.)

4. He failed from first to last to counsel and train a subordinate who was for the first time serving as a foreman.

Group comment was to the effect that Smith's mistakes were caused or contributed to by the mistakes of Prentiss and Morton.

Rules of conduct that could be drawn from analysis of this problem are as follows:

1. An executive at any level should get acquainted with his staff (workers responsible to him) and try to gain their confidence.
2. Obtain as many facts as possible before taking action.
3. Then, weigh the facts before taking action.
4. Obtain advice from all possible sources.
5. Maintain an open mind, free of prejudice.
6. Avoid by-passing at any level.
7. Maintain absolute emotional control regardless of provocation.
8. Do not belittle a person.
9. Know human nature and individual differences.
10. Acquire the habit of giving reasons why.
11. Establish *fair and just* penalties for offenses.
12. Exercise firmness in executing decisions.
13. No foreman or other executive should personally perform an act that has been included in specific instructions or orders to a subordinate. To do so is to lose face.
14. Every executive has a moral obligation to counsel and advise his subordinates.
15. He should anticipate emergencies which are typical of many others and which may happen; then plan how these

emergencies would be best handled. Develop ability to retain self-control in emergencies and to make right decisions even under pressure.

Rules are useless if not followed. In order to help individuals to acquire habits of conduct in human relations that are in keeping with the rules previously listed, the following steps to be taken by each individual are recommended:

1. Keep the minutes of this conference and its rules of conduct in a convenient place and read them frequently. (The leader recommends three times each week for 12 weeks, then not less frequently than once per month, or indefinitely.)

2. Check up on oneself, *i.e.*, analyze oneself and conduct with this list of rules as a measuring stick.

3. Obtain honest opinions of others regarding our conduct. "Others" include:

a. Your associates *b.* Your supervisor *c.* Your subordinates	require that a relationship of mutual confidence and respect be established

4. Attend classes or conferences in human-relations subjects.

5. Read widely on the subject.

Conclusion: This case problem proved most interesting. It also can be helpful in at least two ways. First, you leaders can lead similar conferences and can aid many, many persons to improved human relations. Second, by our own sincere adoption of these rules and making their use habitual, we can make ourselves and others happier. A greater measure of happiness can be achieved by us and those who work with us. We need no higher authority to approve our rules. It is in our hands. Happiness is not a commonplace thing. It is worth striving for, it can be won.

By ______________________
Conference Leader

TEACHERS' CONFERENCE SERIES
CONFERENCE REPORT

Dec. 9, 1947

Problem: Is it advisable to keep students on the school campus during the noon hour?

Objectives:

1. To list advantages to

   a. Business district
   b. Teachers
   c. Students

2. To list disadvantages to

   a. Business district
   b. Teachers
   c. Students

3. To analyze and/or evaluate findings to determine the advisability of the ruling.

Opening Statement: A school like Tech, located practically in the heart of a city, has problems that schools in outlying residential districts do not have. One of our most pressing problems at Tech has been whether or not a noon hour "off the campus" rule is desirable.

Definitions: "Off the campus" means off school property. (Tech school property includes three boys' annexes scattered over several blocks.)

"Business district" refers to area containing business establishments.

"Teachers" includes the instructors, the deans or coordinators, and the director.

"Students" means both boys and girls. (But it must be understood that girls are not the problem the boys are because they are housed only in the main building.)

"Advisability" means prudent, expedient. You will notice, nothing has been mentioned about *enforcement.* We feel that is a distinct and separate *problem.* (To be taken up *if* it is found *advisable* to have such a rule.)

It might be well to state that we should think first of the students' welfare, second, the teachers (as defined), and last, the business district.

Discussion: In discussing the advisability of keeping the students on the school campus during the noon hour, we listed the apparent advantages to the business district.

1. Store employees (especially the store spotters or detectives) would not be required to be more alert due to an influx of students "just looking around."
2. This rule would lessen traffic congestion, with its accompanying hazards to pedestrians and motorists.
3. Restaurants would be less crowded when business people must obtain their lunches.
4. Less litter due to thoughtlessness and carelessness in disposing of lunch wrappings, etc.
5. Gangs in pool halls, etc., not so apt to become a problem to the law.
6. Less bedlam.

This sixth advantage of the rule to the business district seems, at first glance, out of place. However, the thought was that streets and stores would be less disturbed by boys and girls who were (as they say) "getting a breath of freedom" for a few minutes.

We next discussed and listed the advantages to the teachers (note definition above). There seemed to be only two major advantages, so far as the school was concerned, that were advanced and listed during this conference. There may have been others thought of but not expressed.

1. It would mean fewer tardy cases because most of the students would not be off the campus during lunch period.
2. Likewise, fewer truancies because it would lessen the temptation to stay away from school during the afternoon due to stimuli they may have received while wandering around town (such as noticing movie programs, etc.)

When we listed the advantages to the student of being kept at the school during the noon hour, we found three.

1. Students would save money on their lunches and would spend less for knickknacks.

2. They would get more wholesome food at the school cafeteria.

3. The rule would help in keeping the students who are "followers of the gang" out of places not desirable for youth.

One supporter of the rule argued that the more times a pupil is tardy, the more that pupil has a tendency to become habitually so; hence any rule or policy of the school that keeps tardiness down is an advantage to the student. This advantage seemed not strong enough to be listed.

In listing the disadvantages to the three groups concerned, we start again with the business district. After quite a lot of discussion, trying to get some major advantages, we finally could list only one, namely:

1. Stores would lose more or less business because the students would no longer shop for parents, pay bills, and buy things they would be attracted to while loitering around.

It was quite a different story when we started to list the reasons why teachers would rather just dismiss the pupils at noon, as they would if in some outlying residential district. The disadvantages to the teachers of keeping the students on the campus were as follows:

1. Too much noise and disturbance in halls, shops, office, and classrooms. Especially since boys' classes are in session during girls' lunch hour and girls' classes while boys are at lunch.

2. More noon-hour duty for those concerned in order to try to alleviate some of the above noise.

3. Some teachers and coordinators feel "police duty" is necessary when they meet a few pupils who disregard the rule and go to town anyway.

4. "Police duty" is rounding up those who defy the rule.

(Hard to tell whether a student is going to or from an annex.)

5. Increases duties of coordinators and office in determining whether excuses to run errands during the noon hour are legitimate or otherwise.

In listing the disadvantages to the student in keeping them on the campus during noon hour, we find we have four, which were considered of much importance even though briefly stated.

1. Restricts individual freedom too much.
2. Gives less training in self-control.
3. Makes students feel inferior.
4. Makes students feel resentful.

We then came to the final step of our problem, to analyze and/or evaluate our findings to determine the advisability of the ruling at Tech. As we mentioned in our introductory statement, we were to think *first* of the students' welfare, *second* of the teachers (as defined), and *last* of the business district (as defined).

We placed our list of advantages to the business district next to the list of disadvantages and found in analyzing and evaluating them that, to the business district, it was more advantageous to keep the students at the school during noon hour.

We placed our lists side by side for the teachers and found upon analyzing and evaluating them that it was more to the disadvantage of the teachers and school to have such a ruling.

Likewise, on placing our lists of advantages and disadvantages to the students side by side, again weighing and evaluating, we found it was disadvantageous to the students to have such a ruling.

Conclusion: We considered the welfare of the students, teachers, and business district in that order of importance. Since the students' and teachers' lists of *disadvantages* outweighed the *advantages* in value, and only in the case of the business district were these findings the opposite, it seems advisable *not* to have such a ruling.

In summing up our findings, one of the group asked, by vote of hands, how many had come to the conference with their minds already made up. The resulting verbal response took up quite a lot of time and caused the director finally to state, "Although there may have been some who seemed prejudiced, the conference, I am sure, has tended to crystallize our thinking." One member stated she had definitely taken a different attitude toward the problem as a result of the meeting.

By ____________________
Conference Leader

TEACHERS' CONFERENCE SERIES
CONFERENCE REPORT

Nov. 25, 1947

Problem: How can extracurricular activities be apportioned equitably among the teachers of our school?

Objectives:

1. To understand what is meant by extracurricular activities, and to list a number of such activities.
2. To determine what the qualifications are for these activities.
3. To suggest or recommend how to identify the persons possessing the minimum qualifications for these activities.
4. To recommend a plan for apportioning the activity assignments equitably.

Opening Statement: It was agreed by the conferees that we do have responsibilities and opportunities for service outside of duties of curriculum, administration, or teaching. There are moral, if not legal, obligations for the school staff to assist in the extracurricular activities of the students. These extracurricular activities of the students supplement the training received in the various courses of the curriculum. Without these activities the students are less adequately trained to replace their teachers, the businessmen, the government officials, and all of the persons who do worth-while work and render service to the society in which we live. Nonparticipation by the teacher or other staff member in these extracurricular activities is, in most cases, a shirking of a responsibility to the youth of our society.

Discussion: The first discussion step was to arrive at a common understanding of what is meant by extracurricular activities, and to this end a representative list was made as follows:

1. Leadership or sponsorship of the Hi-Y Club.
2. Leadership or sponsorship of the Y-Teens.

3. Leadership or sponsorship of the cheer leaders.
4. Leadership or sponsorship of the monitors.
5. Leadership of the student council.
6. Leadership of the Junior Red Cross.
7. Leadership of the Tigrus Club.
8. Leadership of the safety council.
9. Stage manager for student dramatics.
10. Chaperoning at student social affairs.
11. Sponsorship of visual education.
12. Library management.
13. Special problems committees.
14. Sponsorship of school paper.
15. Sponsorship of school annual.

During the building of this list, reference was made to dictionary definitions, which it is unnecessary to repeat here, since they are readily available.

There was discussion regarding whether extracurricular meant noncontractual. There seemed to be a definite opinion that while in a few cases some extracurricular activities are contractual, most of them are not contractual.

The second step taken in the conference discussion was to list some major qualifications to be met by those staff persons participating in extracurricular activities. The list follows:

1. Willingness to work.
2. Willingness to cooperate (not quite the same as item 1; it means willingness to work with others, and to consider their wishes and convenience).
3. Interest in the activity.
4. A liking for boys and girls.
5. Management ability.
6. Dependability.
7. Availability (available time not yet filled).

In addition to the qualifications recorded, a point was made that assignment to or participation in an activity need not necessarily be in line with the individual's professional specialization. This is a significant fact in appraising the various qualifications.

Step 3 in the discussion was intended to deal with discovering the individuals who possessed the needed qualifications. There was tacit agreement that for a given extracurricular activity some individuals could qualify while others could not, or at least some persons would have less than a desirable minimum of qualifications. In the discussion it was tacitly agreed that some individual or group have the responsibility of seeing that the extracurricular activities were properly sponsored or led by a school staff member. This individual or group would then consider what combination of qualifications a given activity might require and would next make a list of staff members who possessed these qualifications in minimum degree. (No mention was made regarding how the qualifications were to be measured.)

Step 4 in the discussion was the most important, and all the preceding discussion was intended to uncover data to aid the discussion group in reaching a conclusion for step 4.

It early became apparent that, unless an activity was paid for, filling of assignments depends upon the willingness and consent of the appointee. Authority to enforce acceptance is lacking. In this connection, a suggestion was made that participation in extracurricular activities could be contractual, the details to be worked out by the administrator and the staff members. The suggestion did not meet with much favor.

After considerable discussion it became evident that participation in extracurricular activities would probably continue to be on a voluntary basis. However, the administrator could use moral persuasion, pointing out the need and the staff members' moral obligations. Other staff members could add the weight of their opinion, pointing out that willing workers would be overburdened in carrying their own load plus that of workers who persisted in shirking their moral obligations to help carry the load.

At this point the conference discussion was terminated.

Conclusion: The net results of this discussion served to show that this conference problem is not easily solved. No plan to change present procedure was proposed. The chief recommendation seemed to be in the direction of increasing the moral pressure on persons who are reluctant to carry their share of the load.

The leaders' concluding suggestion is that other conference groups discuss this problem and publish the results. Also, a committee might be appointed to investigate how this problem is met in other school organizations, and to report findings to this organization.

By ________________________
Conference Leader

TEACHERS' CONFERENCE SERIES
CONFERENCE REPORT

Nov. 13 and Dec. 4, 1947

Problem: In considering the introduction of an individual appraisal (merit rating) program for teachers, what items or factors should first be considered?

Objectives:

1. To understand what individual appraisal is.
2. To list the items or factors which seem pertinent to the problem and which should be helpful in making recommendations.

    a. For or against adoption of a plan.
    b. For a general outline of an acceptable plan.

3. To decide upon some workable method to evaluate the items previously listed.

Opening Statement: Industrial managements (some of them) are using two companion tools, each of which is necessary in properly rewarding an individual for services rendered.

The first is job evaluation, which is a measurement of the factors that enter into a job and then comparing the sum total of factors for a given job with the sum totals for other jobs. It rates a job with other jobs. It is *job* rating, not a rating of individuals.

The second tool is individual appraisal, which is a measurement of the performance of an individual on a given job, plus an appraisal of his or her personal qualities. Individuals vary in accomplishment and in personal qualities. To pay all persons on the same job the same wages does not recognize the individual differences mentioned. That is why there is a growing demand for both tools, and not just one.

However, it has been difficult to arrive at acceptable and

workable plans for individual appraisal. So many have been poorly constructed and administered that in general this tool is in question, or even in disrepute. Yet the idea is sound. And it is as sound for school organizations as for industry. Individuals both in school and in industry are demanding a recognition of individual improvement and of individual attainment.

It should, then, be profitable for us to take a look at individual appraisal, to discuss it to determine whether it really does offer us advantages not now enjoyed, and, in discussing it, to identify the factors that affect the planning for such a program.

Discussion: The first objective of this conference calls for a definition of individual appraisal. The definition is in four parts as follows:

Individual appraisal is

1. A tool for measuring individual accomplishment on an assigned job or task.

2. A tool for appraising desirable individual qualities and qualifications, for appraising undesirable qualities, and for comparing the two lists.

3. A tool for discovering potential ability or qualities not demanded on the present job, but valuable on other jobs.

4. A tool to discover how best to develop an individual, *i.e.*, to discover those things which an individual may lack and which he may be aided to acquire.

The second objective asked for a list of factors which are pertinent to the problem and which would be helpful in making recommendations as to whether such a plan should be adopted, and, if adopted, in making recommendations for a general outline or plan. The following items were listed:

1. Benefits that might be expected as a result of having an individual appraisal program.

a. Increased efficiency of individuals.
b. Better mutual understanding.

c. Recognition that there are differences in individuals.

d. Self-appraisal would be stimulated.

e. There might be established standards as a basis for advancement and/or adjustment.

f. Provides incentive for self-improvement.

g. Indirectly but significantly the school pupils will benefit, and so should the community.

h. The school board would be helped to do a better job.

2. Possible objections and/or difficulties that probably would be involved.

a. Fears of individual teachers that the plan will not work, or will be wrongly administered, which would be to the individual's disadvantage.

b. Jealousy among teachers.

c. Lack of understanding (by teachers) of the mechanics of the program, therefore difficulty in selling the program.

d. Difficulty in measuring rated factors, rather than guessing at the ratings.

e. Pedantic attitude of some educators.

f. Unwillingness of some teachers to have a pay scale based on individual appraisal.

3. Job performance factors that might be used in the plan.

a. Attendance.

b. Punctuality.

c. Quality of the teacher's daily preparation.

d. Degree of understanding of children and success in management of children.

e. Ability (success) in relations with parents.

f. Success in relations with fellow teachers.

g. Participation in problems and activities outside the classroom.

h. Success in "putting across" (having the students learn) the subjects taught by the teacher.

i. Success in relations with one's administrators and supervisors.

j. Willingness and ability to support school policies.

k. Extent of personal and professional improvement.

l. Efficiency in desk work.

4. Personal qualities that might be measured.

a. Cooperativeness.

b. Friendliness.

c. Judgment ability, including a good sense of values.

d. Loyalty (to one's beliefs, to school policies, to students, to associates, to administrators and supervisors).

e. Appearance.

f. Initiative.

g. Sense of humor.

h. Health, physical and mental.

i. Enthusiasm.

j. Personal integrity.

k. Persistence.

The thought was expressed that the quality of "wearing well" was desirable. In discussing this item, it was thought that a person rating high in the items listed would undoubtedly wear well.

5. What measuring devices should be used to measure the job factors and personal qualities included in the plan?

a. The ratings should be accurate measurements, rather than opinions, estimates, or approximations. Only ratings or measurements that can be proved to the satisfaction of the person appraised are worth while. If a factor cannot be measured with reasonable accuracy, it should be excluded from the appraisal plan. In most cases, a special measuring plan will have to be constructed by persons with experience in this work.

6. How often should the appraisal of individuals be made?

   a. The appraisal procedure would be regular and continuous over the period of a school year, and a summary of the appraisal on all factors would be prepared toward the close of the school year.

   b. At any time there may be, and often there should be, personal interviews between a teacher and those responsible for part of the appraisal procedure. This means in most cases the teacher and the person to whom the teacher is directly responsible.

7. Who should make teacher individual appraisal?

   a. Probably the best plan would be to have a committee or group including the person to whom the teacher is directly responsible (in many cases this would be the school principal), the supervisor, the superintendent, and any other appropriate person. The reason for preferring a small group rather than one person, even though that one person is the teacher's immediate superior, is that the appraisals may be more accurate, more impersonal, and will be better accepted by individual teachers.

8. Who should present the appraisal results or summary to the teacher?

   a. The best choice for this responsibility is the person to whom the teacher in question is directly responsible.

The third conference objective raised the question of how the various factors in the appraisal plan should be weighted.

There was no attempt to weight the factors suggested for the appraisal plan. One reason for not doing so was that the list of factors presented included more than would actually be used, and hence the time was not appropriate for this weighting process. Also, there would be insufficient time available in this conference to do so.

It was suggested and agreed to that the most desirable method for weighting the factors would be by a democratic vote of all persons included in the appraisal plan. This vote would be planned for and conducted by chosen school administrators, but without dictation to the persons voting on the weights of factors.

Conclusion: The purpose of holding this conference was to present information, to stimulate discussion and thinking, and to clarify ideas in the minds of participants. This has been accomplished. It was not intended to use the items developed in the conference in making recommendations at this time. Later, the items developed in the conference should greatly aid in making recommendations.

By ______________________

Conference Leader

TEACHERS' CONFERENCE SERIES
CONFERENCE REPORT

Feb. 10, 1948

Problem: How can daily attendance of the pupils of the Riverside School be improved?

Objectives:

1. To become familiar with the excuses that pupils at the Riverside School give as reasons for absence from school.
2. To determine which of the excuses listed are legitimate excuses for staying out of school, and which are the ones about which something could and should be done by the school.
3. To suggest and recommend some things that might be done in an effort to eliminate an undue amount of daily absence.

Definition: The group defined "legitimate" excuses for absence from school as being those that pertained to the health of the child. If a pupil is physically, mentally, or emotionally upset, he should not be expected to attend school at that time.

Dicussion: At the opening of the discussion, it was conceded by all the conferees that statements such as the following were frequently being made: "Such and such a child is absent too much" and "So and so is absent unnecessarily."

For that reason the group felt there was a need to *do* something about the situation. It was agreed that it would be helpful to first examine the teachers' weekly absence reports for this past school year, and together make a representative list of excuses given for absence. Then would follow an analysis of the excuses listed in an effort to determine which of them were not legitimate excuses for absence from school, with suggestions and recommendations as to some things that could be done to eliminate absence not due to illness of the pupil himself. The group felt that in a school district such as that of Riverside School, where many pupils come from broken homes, and where many pupils come from families in the very low income brackets, making it necessary for the mother in the family to be employed outside the home, the school must assume a greater responsibility for regular attendance of its pupils.

Attention was called to cases in which it had been necessary for a pupil to repeat a grade, even though he was a capable one, merely because he had missed out on the drill or the teacher's explanations given during his frequent absences. Then, too, lack of interest in school evidenced in certain children could be traced partly to irregular attendance at school.

With the above as introduction to the problem, the group set about making the list of excuses for absence, with the following as the result:

1. Overslept; clock stopped; stayed up too late.
2. Out of town; visiting; had company; vacationing.
3. Toothache.
4. Headache; fever.
5. Earache.
6. Sore throat.
7. Cold; "flu."
8. No dry clothes to wear; no clean clothes.
9. Shoes being repaired.
10. Shopping for clothes.
11. Mother ill.
12. Took care of younger brothers and sisters.

The first step in the discussion of the problem, that of making the list of excuses given, was disposed of by the group in the shortest amount of time possible in order to have ample time left in which to suggest remedies for the situation, which the conferees felt was the important thing.

Next, the discussion centered around the excuses that should be acceptable for the pupil absence. The group took the attitude that, in some few instances, any of the above listed 12 excuses might possibly be considered valid excuses for a pupil's being absent from school, but that they would not be acceptable if they occurred frequently. For example, a pupil might miss school *once* due to the fact that the clock stopped, but if that child were out of school once every week or two for such a reason, something would definitely need to be done about the situation, and a visit to the home would probably be in order in an effort to secure parent cooperation in such a matter.

However, the group agreed that generally a child should be absent from classes only for personal ailments. This led to the expression by the group that even some of the illness could be eliminated with proper efforts. For example, it was found that a number of children were absent from school due to toothache. It was pointed out that loss of time from school for this reason could be greatly reduced by the school and home cooperating on solving this problem.

The third and final step in this discussion was that of listing a few of the things this group felt that they would like to do immediately in an effort to improve the attendance of the pupils enrolled in the Riverside School. Following is the list, minus many of the details suggested because of the limited space here:

1. More home contacts with pupils' parents, either by principal, nurse, or teacher, in an effort to better understand the whole child.

2. Requiring of notes from parents in regard to all pupil absence.

3. Renewed effort to stimulate interest in pupil himself for being responsible for good school attendance.

4. Adjusting of the curriculum in such a way that each and every child could feel that he was making some real progress every day.

5. Keeping the atmosphere of the schoolroom a happy and interesting one at all times, so that pupil will want to be present at school of his own accord.

6. Keep P.T.A. members attendance-conscious by short monthly reports to them in regard to some phase of school attendance.

7. Use sixth-grade school newspaper for publicizing such items as the effect of irregular school attendance on one's school accomplishments, etc.

8. Stress good health habits as part of the school curriculum for every grade, kindergarten through sixth grade.

9. Provide some free health services for pupils whose parents cannot afford to give them to their children. (Along this line, it might be interesting to note here that between 30 and 40 pupils of the Riverside School have received, or are receiving at the present time, free dental care through the generosity of a local sorority.)

10. Teachers make a special effort to have a good attendance record themselves, as an example to their pupils.

Conclusion: As a result of this conference the conferees expressed the opinion that they were greatly impressed with two facts: first, that there is a great deal of unnecessary absence among the pupils of the Riverside School; and, secand, that each teacher is, to a large degree, responsible for the regular attendance of her pupils. Not that any one teacher should be expected to do all the needful things in correcting the situation, but she should be alert and attendance-conscious, and ever watchful for any opportunity that presents itself for the doing of something constructive along this line, either by the principal, the nurse, or herself.

The leader of this conference was greatly gratified by the wholesome attitude displayed by the group in recognizing that a successful solution of the problem would definitely necessitate a self-analysis on the part of each teacher involved to determine whether or not certain omissions or commissions on her part might not be indirectly responsible for pupil-absence in her room.

Finally, it was agreed by the discussion group that from time to time during the remainder of the school year, it would be worth while to hold further conferences on this problem.

By ____________________

Principal, Riverside School
Conference Leader

PRINCIPALS' CONFERENCE SERIES
CONFERENCE REPORT

Jan. 28, 1948

Problem: What can we as principals and superintendents do to efficiently control class interruptions?

Objectives:

1. To list and classify activities and duties that fall in the category of class interruptions. The activities and duties include

   a. Those relative to regular school organization and administration.
   b. Those relative to school fund raising.
   c. Those relative to community drives and campaigns.

2. To list ways and means by which the principal can be more proficient in organizing and controlling these activities to make them less interrupting.

Definition: All activities or projects that take time from the planned activities of the teacher's day are included in this conference as "class interruptions."

Opening Statement:

> Go slowly, go slowly, O Time, have mercy on me,
> Let me get everything done before it is three!
> Let no interruptions mar this peaceful day.
> Let me follow my schedule, just once, I do pray.
> Let no one come knocking at my classroom door,
> Give me a day with my children, I beg and implore.
> Go slowly, go slowly, O Time, have mercy on me,
> Let me get everything done before it is three!

"Class interruptions" is merely a polite way of speaking of being annoyed and bothered when trying to do a definite task. No problem can be efficiently completed within a given time if continuous interruptions are permitted. I'm sure that we all agree that many of the interrupting activities that we have are valuable in themselves and, no doubt, would not be classified as interruptions if properly controlled and organized, while others may not justifiably interrupt regular classroom or schoolday time.

It is the purpose of this conference to call to our attention the various interrupting duties and activities that our teachers have to confront while doing their regular duty as classroom teachers, and then to develop ways and means to control these interruptions so that they may be held to a minimum or be so organized and placed in the program that they do not interfere with regular classroom teaching, but become part of it.

Discussion: The first objective of this conference calls for a list of interruptions relative to regular school organization and administration. They are as follows:

1. Means of distributing bulletins.
2. Teacher and principal announcements to pupils.
3. Pupil problems and counseling.
4. Parent visits.
5. Telephone calls and other emergency information.
6. Student council.
7. Religious instruction.
8. Maintenance.
9. School assemblies, regular and special.
10. Assembly preparations.
11. Class trips and excursions.
12. Traveling exhibits, room to room.
13. Tournaments and other athletic activities.
14. Early dismissals.
15. Room parties.
16. School festivals, operettas, etc.
17. Junior Red Cross activities.
18. Safety patrol.
19. Fire drills.
20. Health examinations.
21. Band.

22. Special teacher projects.
23. P.T.A. programs.

The second part of the first objective calls for a list of interruptions relative to school fund raising. They are as follows:

1. Wastepaper drives.
2. Magazine subscription drives.
3. Movies and other shows.
4. Carnivals.
5. P.T.A. fund-raising activities.
6. Rental collections.
7. All other sales.

The third part of the first objective calls for a list of interruptions relative to community drives and campaigns. They are as follows:

1. City community chest.
2. Red Cross.
3. March of Dimes.
4. Cancer.
5. Various ticket drives.
6. Parades.

The second objective of this conference calls for a list of ways and means to aid the principal in becoming more proficient in controlling these interrupting activities. They are as follows:

1. Have a scheduled time for routine bulletins to be in teachers' mailboxes in the office.

2. Have a definite deadline time for information that is to be sent out by bulletin the following day to be in the office.

3. Have a scheduled time in the program each day for teachers to distribute and discuss this bulletin information with pupils.

4. No interruption without office approval.

5. Principals should practice strict control—learn to say, "No."

6. Schedule all special teachers in same quarter of day, when possible—then stay within the program.

7. It was agreed that our activities period each day was a good means for controlling many interruptions.

8. Band lessons and safety patrol duties should be scheduled for study periods when possible.

9. Confine excursions to class groups.

10. Early dismissals should be discouraged.

11. There was difference of opinion in regard to seventh- and eighth-grade tournaments—probably yes, with adequate help.

12. Some principals favored a more uniform time for afternoon dismissals for each of the lower grades—difference of opinion.

13. Paper drives should be held at a definite limited time, with provision for special activity work for nonparticipants.

14. Should concentrate school drives to shorter periods of time.

15. A school community chest was suggested.

By ____________________
Conference Leader

PRINCIPALS' CONFERENCE SERIES
CONFERENCE REPORT

Jan. 8, 1948

Problem: What can we do to maintain regular daily attendance of school children?

Premise of Discussion:

1. Regular daily attendance of pupils is essential in order to attain
   - *a.* Educational progress of pupils enrolled.
   - *b.* Financial gain to school city. (State aid determined by average daily attendance.)

Objectives:

1. To determine who is responsible for good school attendance.
2. To list problems involved in maintaining regular daily attendance.
3. To list steps to be taken to solve the attendance problems listed.

Discussion: Who is responsible for maintaining regular daily attendance of pupils?

1. Parents.
2. Superintendent of schools.
3. Board of education.
4. Teachers.
5. Principals.
6. Health department.
7. Attendance and child welfare department.
8. Office clerks.
9. Pupil himself.
10. General public.
11. Outside agencies, such as courts and welfare agencies, legal and voluntary.

Comment: From the school's position, the entire school staff must share the responsibility of keeping ing pupils in regular attendance.

Problems Involved in Maintaining Good School Attendance:

1. Parent and public education—develop wholesome attitude toward public education by means of good public relations program.
2. Curriculum—adequate and adapted and interpreted to child's learning.
3. Health of pupils—provide functional health services.
4. Home—provide means to investigate and assist in removal of barriers to good school attendance.
5. Pupil attitudes—cultivate in school and home.
6. Conflicting programs—extra and outside activities.
7. Pupil work experiences—opportunity and demand for pupil services.
8. Pupil living habits—late hours, excess activities.
9. Personality conflicts—among pupils, teachers, parents.
10. Lack of school-staff cooperation—individuals and departments.
11. Need of special services—physical and mental health clinics, pupil counselors, etc.

Steps to be Taken in Solving Attendance Problems:

1. Teacher—what can she do?
   - *a.* Make schoolwork attractive and interesting.
   - *b.* Understand pupils—gauge pupils' learning level and interests, teach pupils, not subjects.
   - *c.* Be attendance-conscious—encourage pupils.
   - *d.* Make home contacts—meet parents, home visits.
   - *e.* Radiate learning atmosphere—classroom enthusiasm.
   - *f.* Be alert to pupil problems and make referrals at proper time and to right source for assistance.

g. Acquire pupil's respect—make pupil want to emulate wholesome attitudes and conduct.

2. Principal—what can he or she do to solve problems?

a. Emphasize importance of regular attendance to teachers, pupils, and parents.
b. Principals can demand that attendance reports be in on time, and must be accurate.
c. Follow-up—frequent re-emphasis on attendance and spot special cases.
d. Make occasional home visits—meet parents.
e. Promote school atmosphere—encourage and promote pupil interest in school. School will not rise beyond leadership of top individual.
f. Coordinate efforts of staff—utilize greatest training, talent and interest of teachers wherever possible and firmly and openly support and encourage good work and good judgment. Will promote teacher-pupil morale.
g. Referrals—exhaust means for solution at school first—then determine when, where, and to whom referral should be made with information and suggestions in solution of problem.

3. What can superintendents of schools do to maintain good attendance in the school system?

a. Lend support to the efforts of his staff in maintaining regular attendance.
b. Public contacts—interpret and emphasize value of good attendance to community.

4. Department of attendance and child welfare.

a. Give prompt attention to referrals.
b. Process cases beyond solution by local school.
c. Enforce attendance laws.
d. Receive and check school attendance reports.
e. Handle extraordinary discipline cases.

f. Protect welfare of child—child labor, child neglect, child abuse, pupil adjustment, and aid to indigent cases.

5. What the health department can do.

a. Provide good prevention program.
b. Discover, treat and refer health cases.
c. Make home calls—advise parents.
d. Cooperate with individuals, organizations, and departments of school system.
e. Cooperate with local doctors and other agencies.

6. What can parents do?

a. Cooperate with schools—will need guidance, counsel, and encouragement from school staff.
b. Display interest in child's progress in school and school activities.

7. Outside agencies—cooperate with schools. Township trustee, Department of Public Welfare, juvenile court, Red Cross, general relief agency, and civic clubs and organizations.

Comment: These agencies can encourage school attendance by rendering material aid contingent on school attendance, by consulting with schools where aid is needed, by providing means for extra services to pupils, and by using school history of pupils in making decisions, especially in court cases.

Conclusion: To maintain a high standard of school attendance among pupils is the responsibility of every member of the school personnel. Parents and citizens of the community must likewise assume a large share of the responsibility. The solution of the problems involved demand cooperation and understanding of all concerned. Attendance is a problem that necessitates perpetual emphasis and re-emphasis throughout the school year. The school will serve the community in direct proportion to the extent that its constituency will be present to profit by its academic offerings and other services. Regular attendance is a first essential.

It is planned, therefore, to hold further conferences on this problem, properly spaced as to time. Also, each member of this group reaffirms his and her willingness and intention to do whatever is possible to further the cause of better attendance of school pupils.

By ____________________

Director of Attendance and
Child Welfare
Conference Leader

INDEX